D0384100

A Millionaire's
Common Sense Approach
to Wealth

A Millionaire's Common Sense Approach to Wealth

Dexter Yager
with
Ron Ball

Freedom Distributing Company, Inc.

I thank Ron Ball, a good friend, for his willingness and patience to spend countless hours and endless nights interviewing me for this book. I congratulate his efforts in guiding the direction of my thoughts and organizing them on paper.

Scripture marked TLB is taken from *The Living Bible*, © 1971, owned by assignment by Illinois Regional Bank N. A. (as trustee). Used by permission of Tyndale House Publishers, Inc., Wheaton, Illinois 60189. All rights reserved. Scripture marked NKJV is taken from *The Holy Bible*, New King James Version, © 1979, 1980, 1982 by Thomas Nelson, Inc., Publishers.

Cover photo by Dennis Nodine/Dennis Nodine Photography, Charlotte, NC

1   2   3   4   5   6   7   8   95   94   93   92   91   90   89

To my parents, Leonard and Gertrude Yager—
who taught me basic money management
and the value of a dollar.

To my wife, Birdie, and my seven children—
who in the early days,
when we were really broke,
became the necessity to manage effectively
what little money we had.

CONTENTS

PREFACE

For years I've taught people about common-sense financial principles, on which I've built my life. Through those years I've counseled thousands of people concerning their finances. I've learned that common sense is uncommon and that too little emphasis is paid to the management of money. Even as a child I was so ingrained with these principles that they became a natural part of my life. This I owe to my parents' guidance. As a result, I've been blessed with success.

This book gives me a chance to share with others this common-sense approach to financial prosperity and wealth. I hope those that need it most will now have it in their hands and be able to absorb it, understand it, and most of all put it into daily practice for their own success.

Dexter Yager
June 26, 1989

Part I
UNDERSTANDING
FINANCIAL
PROSPERITY

ONE
MISCONCEPTIONS ABOUT MONEY AND MATERIALISM

A man once said to me, "I'm always sharing new business opportunities and visions of success with my friends, but they continually accuse me of materialism. They're always on my back, always after me, saying I'm materialistic. All I want to do is make a better life for my family. Tell me, am I materialistic?"

It's a common question. Is attaining financial security for people you love materialism? Is paying your bills on time materialism? Is guaranteeing a comfortable, happy future for your spouse and children materialism?

Well, let me tell you—NO! Providing a good life for your spouse and family is not materialism. Yet people all over America have a warped perspective on this, and it keeps people like you from achieving what you ought to achieve.

Many of us are church members, and we're particularly sensitive to the danger of becoming materialistic. But do you know that less than eighty percent of all church members tithe their income? Do you realize that most church facilities in this country are owned by banks and financial institutions and that many churches are enormously in debt? Pastors often are among the lowest paid professionals in our communities. This isn't right; it's not biblical; it's not from God.

We've got to understand what materialism actually is. Materialism is not the same as positive achievement or building financial security for your family or success in life. That's not materialism. Materialism is a preoccupation with material things, the worship of money and possessions, a life that is controlled by financial considerations.

I'm here to tell you that many people, out of their fear of materialism, are playing right into the hands of materialism. By failing to master their money, they allow it to master them. In fact the only way to overcome materialism is to lead a life that is financially free.

FIVE ATTITUDES TOWARD MONEY

I have identified five basic perspectives that most people have toward money. Not all of these are right perspectives, and several are negative, but these are the common viewpoints, and they keep people from a healthy, productive understanding of money and wealth.

1. Fear. Believe it or not, many people are afraid of money and of what they think it represents. More specifically, people are afraid of capitalism. Do you realize there are actually people who blame money for poverty? They blame wealthy people for the poor people. They say that if all these wealthy people weren't consuming so much and spending so much there wouldn't be so many poor people. I want to tell you that's completely illogical. In fact, it is the wealthy, achieving people who produce jobs.

Capitalism is often blamed for poverty, but I believe that it is socialism that creates poverty. My personal definition of socialism is that it is stealing from those who've earned it to give to those who don't deserve it. Socialism is essentially just that— stealing. It works as a demotivator, and it's responsible for keeping millions of Americans at or below the poverty level. Now isn't it interesting that we are seeing socialist and communist societies around the world finally come face to face with the economic and spiritual bankruptcy of socialism and begin to adopt some forms of capitalism? They won't admit that's what they are doing, but underneath the jargon of *glasnost* and social incentives are some old-fashioned principles of capitalism.

Yet in America many people are reluctant to embrace capitalism because they've been taught to be afraid of it. They've learned, wrongly, that it is responsible for the condition of poverty.

I'm not saying you never help someone who is in genuine need. Compassion is essential. But you don't really help people solve their financial problems by eliminating those—the wealthy—who don't have financial problems. Yes, you should be a giver and a contributor to other people and organizations that help other people, but many people have a great fear of money, of capitalism, and of wealthy people that is irrational and demotivating.

2. *Anger.* People blame money for all of their problems and they get angry toward it. Now, this is similar to being afraid of it, but it's a little different—it's a little more militant. Anger is an aggressive attitude toward money.

Sometimes this is caused by a person's bad feelings about his job. If a person hates his job, but must work in order to make money, he tends to transfer his anger to money itself. He is angry that he has to work to make money. People get angry about the bills they have to pay, or about the taxes that the government takes out of their paychecks, or about unexpected household expenses that drain the savings account.

I believe that TV force-feeds negative impressions of wealthy people and large businesses and corporations. People transfer these false, fictional images into real life. For many people, money is associated with negative things, and people blame money for their problems. People get angry toward money itself, and consequently it becomes difficult for them to understand it adequately enough to be able to use it effectively.

3. *Dependency.* Some people depend on money

more than others. I don't mean just that they need more money, but that they rely on it for psychological reasons. They need it to feel good about themselves, to build up their self-esteem. They see it as an extension of character, a reflection of who they are. If they don't have the right brand of clothing, aren't driving the right car, or aren't living in the right neighborhood, then they get depressed and dejected, and they feel like they're not worth all that much. It's a dependency, maybe like alcohol or compulsive gambling, where a physical thing becomes intertwined with one's self-image. If you need to prove the value and worth of who you are through money and possessions, you're in big trouble.

Several years ago I was looking at a multimillion-dollar investment deal. I had scheduled a meeting with the man who was going to buy this project and was going to let me in, in a small way. He had considerable status. I brought with me some of my friends, among them a dentist, doctors, lawyers, and other people of some standing. They were quite upset with me because I wore Levis and a sweatshirt to the meeting. They, of course, were all dressed up in suits. So we met with this very wealthy man, and after about an hour of discussion, he said, "Well, Dexter, why don't you let your employees go. You and I will finish the talking." He assumed because they were well-dressed that they must be my employees. This wealthy man happened to be in a T-shirt, shorts, and sneakers.

Often you can tell when someone is overdependent on money and on the trappings that money can buy. People who are truly wealthy don't need money to enhance their self-image.

4. *Love.* Some people are controlled by a love of money. They love it so intensely that it becomes a ruthless god. They come to worship money, and that's wrong. It's interesting to me that people who worry about their finances all the time and who struggle constantly to make ends meet are often the people who worship money. And it seems that wealthy people, who don't wrestle with those things so much, accept money for what it is and nothing more—they tend not to worship money. I think it's a matter of whether money controls you or you control it. If it controls you, then it can very easily become a god, a merciless god, and a object of worship.

5. *Guilt.* Right now there is a liberal war against wealth in this country, and there are liberal leaders all over America in the university systems who continually fight what they call the "oppressive perspectives" of capitalism. Yet it's capitalism that generates the money to pay their salaries, to keep their universities open, to keep educational television on the air. It's a terrible contradiction. They say we should feel guilty as Americans because we consume so much of the world's goods. (They fail to say that we also *produce* much of the world's goods.) These attitudes weaken achievement and the sense of personal motivation, which makes people feel guilty for building something and succeeding. One of the great principles of life

is that if you've earned something, it is then a legitimate reward. You shouldn't feel guilty for enjoying it.

I believe these attitudes toward money hold people back from achieving financial success. Not just that, but they hold people back from achieving all that they can be personally. I'm here to tell you that there is no reason to fear money, or harbor anger and resentment toward it, or develop personal dependencies with it, or love and worship it, or feel guilty about using it. Money is a tool that needs to be mastered. It takes skill to use it effectively, but you can develop that skill and make money work for you.

MODERN MONEY MYTHS

In addition to having destructive attitudes about money, many people buy into what I call the Five Modern Money Myths. It amazes me that these myths lie at the heart of the most successful economic system in the history of the world—American capitalism—and that in this great nation we are still laboring under some terrible misconceptions. If that's true of us, what's true of the rest of the world? We're the financial leadership of the world. We need to correct our fuzzy, backward thinking in these areas.

Myth #1: You get money by lucky breaks. This means getting money in what I call "the TV way"— you get a break, you inherit a fortune, you win a lottery. (Do you realize that most people in America right now of lower- and middle-class status believe that the best possibility for getting rich is through a lawsuit? Amazing!) To many people, wealth comes from luck and opportunism. NO! That's a myth. People looking for a lucky break never find it, and they squander all their opportunities for making the most out of what they have. The truth is, you get money by working for it, earning it slowly, steadily building it over many years through saving and investing. You get money by developing disciplined, money-handling habits. You get money by learning not to waste it on lottery tickets.

Myth #2: Money is for spending. One of the basic reasons why young men and women out of college have had such a difficult time is that they have been the lowest percentage of savers in recent history. They have saved money at a lower rate than their parents. They have consumed it at a much higher rate. So the attitude is that money is for right now, for immediate use, for personal pleasure.

But the true perspective on money is that money should serve you, and that you should not be the slave of it. Use your money. Make it work for you, not against you. One of the most helpful books I have ever read on this subject is a tiny paperback entitled *The Richest Man in Babylon.* It teaches you that every penny every day can be made to serve you and work for you and that you cannot over-consume and ever expect to have true wealth.

You see, there is a difference between many wealthy people and many poor people in this country besides the fact that one group has money and the other group doesn't. Sometimes these groups are referred to as the "haves" and the "have-nots," which I think terribly oversimplifies the state of things. The real difference is that many wealthy people have found ways of using money to create their wealth; many poor people spend money as soon as they get it. Now I know this sounds terribly unfair and insensitive, and I know that many poor people are in difficult situations, but nevertheless I believe it's basically true. There are many wealthy people in this country who started out with nothing, at or below poverty level. What has made them different from the others? They've learned that money is not for right now—to be spent and consumed for things that won't last. Rather it is something to be used for the future—to be invested in things that will last.

Myth #3: Getting paid is the same thing as making money. It's not. You can get paid a high salary but still not be making significant money. You see, getting paid and making a profit are two different things. For example, when you work for someone else and you get your paycheck at the end of a week, you are getting paid for a service you have rendered to that company. There is a limit to how much you will get paid; there is a ceiling on your income. They will pay you only so much because the company is taking the big risks in the enterprise, so it gets the big profits. If the company did poorly in a given year, you would still get paid the same amount (assuming the company did not go bankrupt). So the company is taking risks.

So, you see, you're trading your potential to make more money for a job and a life that involves less risk. Which is perfectly fair. But if you want to make a higher profit, you have to take a higher risk. Go into business for yourself. You'll face greater risks, but if you overcome them, you can make a lot more money. Winston Churchill said that the greatest difference between great people and average people is the willingness to take risks. And the bigger the risks, the bigger the potential for profit.

What I'm saying is that most people think that as long as they have a good paycheck, then they're secure financially. But that's not the same thing as making money—it's trading your service and time for a paycheck. If you truly want to make a *profit*, then you need to save, take a risk, and build over the long term.

Myth #4: If you have money, you're rich. No. There is a major difference between money and wealth. Let me explain.

Sure, if you receive a high paycheck, you are getting money. But that's not necessarily wealth. According to Harvard University, true wealth is that which produces a steady, ongoing stream of continuous income. Wealth is when you make money from money.

You see, if you receive a $100,000 salary every year, well, that's wonderful, but if you spend it and squander it and it doesn't produce any more income, what happens to you if you no longer get the check? What happens when it's gone? True wealth is where you build your salary to the point that it produces income itself—steady income for life.

There are systems in America right now where you can build to a certain point that will produce income for life. You need to find a system like that. But the major principle here is to remember that just receiving money is not the same thing as receiving wealth, even if there's a big paycheck involved. Wealth is that which produces a steady, ongoing stream of continuous income.

Myth #5: Becoming wealthy is materialistic. This brings us full circle. We're back to where we started. This is the most serious, damaging myth, because it paints a distorted picture of wealth and personal achievement. It stops men and women from doing and achieving great things in their lives.

In order to understand the materialism myth, you need to understand the definition of materialism. It's a scary word to most people. Materialism is the worship of the material. It is the sincere belief that the true meaning of your life is not in God, or family, or truth, or people, but in your possession of the material. That's the true meaning of materialism. It is the worship of material things. It exists when the *material* is your god, when you bow before its altar day and night. *Ism* means a value system of belief, the belief that the true meaning of your life is found in the material.

Now honestly, are you really a materialist? By that definition, are you a materialist just because you want a better life for your family? Are you a materialist because you would like to have a better, safer car, one that lasts longer? Are you a materialist because you want a house in a better neighborhood where your children can go to a better school? Are you a materialist because you've always loved swimming and you want to put in a swimming pool, and you want your children to bring their friends over so you can supervise their activities? Are you a materialist because you love to see different parts of the world and you've earned enough money to take your family to Australia for two weeks to see that part of the world? I don't think so.

I heard a story once of a Christian woman who was talking to a man who had just lectured on success. The woman remarked that she couldn't dream of new achievements for herself. The lecturer, trying to help her dream new dreams, asked her to tell him what she would really like in life, what she really wanted. She finally conceded, "I want a new swimming pool. I'd love to have a swimming pool. I'd like to work for it, achieve it, make more money this year, and have a swimming pool." The next day she spoke to the lecturer again. She had been consumed with guilt. Some of her friends, who had overheard the conversation the previous day, had pounced on her after the meeting and called her a materialist. The woman was crushed. She felt that she had betrayed her friends and feared she had betrayed God. The lecturer said, "Let me ask you an honest question. You're telling me that because you'd like a swimming pool and you're willing to work for it, that's going to make you a materialist?" She said, "I'm afraid of that." And he replied, "Well, let me ask you another question. When you mentioned the swimming pool, what were your immediate feelings?" She said, "Oh, I was excited! I was motivated to make more money and be a better person and just be better in everything. I was just so motivated by my goal." And then the lecturer said, "There's no way in the world that's materialism. If you want to achieve more and make more money, and do it honestly, that's not materialism. That is honest, legitimate achievement. It's goal setting. That's an honest desire to better your life and yourself. And if you want to be what God made you to be, then becoming better financially is not materialistic— it's fantastic!"

The mistake most people make is in thinking that materialism has to do with the nature of the things you own and acquire. It doesn't. Materialism is an attitude toward the things you own and acquire. Let me explain.

The value of material things is relative. Years ago, a wealthy person was someone who had a television set; today even poor people have one. It used to be that the average family was lucky to own a car; today average families own two. The things you look upon today as being materialistic will ten years from now be considered standard. The value of material things is relative.

What materialism is really all about is an attitude. Some people use things in the wrong way.

As we have seen, sometimes people depend on material things for their self-image. Other times people get priorities out of whack and start to value things more than people, even to the extent of loving things so much that they use people to get them. That's materialism.

When you value material things for what they are and nothing more—as conveniences in life that have relative (and often depreciating) value—you are not being materialistic. With that attitude, it is not necessarily more materialistic to own a swimming pool than not to own one. In fact, it has nothing to do with owning a swimming pool at all. It has to do with a person's attitude toward the swimming pool, what it means to them, and how important it becomes in his life. Consider this scenario: One person owns a swimming pool and another doesn't. It's quite possible that the one who doesn't own the swimming pool desires to own one very much, seeing it as a reflection of his self-image, wanting it to make him more popular in the neighborhood. The one who owns the swimming pool enjoys it because it helps him relax on hot summer nights; he is pleased he owns it, but he has no illusions about its ultimate worth. Now which person is more materialistic? You see, materialism has little to do with "what" and everything to do with "why."

It grieves me to see people get the wrong idea about this. Why? Because this misconception about materialism deters people from becoming tremendously productive in life. Material things motivate us to achieve things that are far greater than the material things themselves. If you fear materialism and have this tremendous concern that you're going to fall into this materialistic trap, you then need to realize that materialism is not the same as achievement. It's not the same at all.

IMAGES OF THE RICH AND FAMOUS

I think one of the real roadblocks to achievement in this country and one of the barriers to an accurate understanding of materialism is the bad image rich and wealthy people have at the hands of the media. In most of our television programs and movies, the rich and wealthy are depicted in negative ways. None of us is immune to the power of these images.

You've watched "Dallas" and "Dynasty" and "LA Law," and that is where you get your image of successful businessperson. Here he is in a pinstripe suit; there she is living in a high-rise condo. And they have no ethical principles. Do you realize that most TV villains of the last ten years have been wealthy, successful businessmen and businesswomen? J.R. Ewing is the image of the successful businessman to most Americans, and too many Americans still believe if you attain a high level of achievement and wealth and success, you got it because you cheated.

Let me tell you something. That image is distorted. I have been privileged to know a number of successful people in my time, people of power and wealth, and they achieved their position and money by hard work, ethical principles, loving people, loving God, and honestly serving the needs of others. They didn't get it by cheating, dishonesty, or immoral behavior. There's no reason in the world that achievement and wealth automatically imply these negative things. Yet these media images give a lot of people an excuse never to succeed and achieve.

There are four major images of the rich and famous that people in this country have developed, several of them through the destructive work of the media. Let me tell you about them.

Image #1—Wealthy people as outlaws and criminals. I remember the popular movie *Wall Street.* It presented the wealth-producing establishment of America. In this program you have a picture of corruption, cheating, lying, and stealing—a very gloomy picture. Outlaws and criminals. Now I heard of one man who works for an investment firm on Wall Street. He said that much of that picture is not true, but that there's just enough truth in it to give people the idea that outlaws and criminals operate our great wealth-producing establishment in New York. Consequently many people view all of the rich and all of the wealthy as outlaws and criminals, and they are convinced that these people have produced their wealth through immorality, lying, cheating, and stealing.

Image #2—The wealthy as arrogant snobs. I read about a woman who took $2 million to redecorate and renovate a co-op apartment off of Central Park in New York City. She spent more than $1 million on marble for the foyer, the inner walls of her bedroom, and the living room. She explained to some friends that she had to spend that kind of money or all her other friends would reject her. They would not want to be friends with her if she did not decorate her apartment lavishly, in keeping with their level of wealth. This woman also put in a special, custom-built icebox beside her bathroom tub. She didn't have this icebox so she could have something cold to drink when she was having a warm bath. She wanted an ice box so she could chill her cologne! She said that all of her friends agreed there is nothing worse than getting out of a hot bath and reaching for your cologne, and finding it lukewarm. So she spent a lot of money to chill her cologne.

Now, it's not so much her expenditures that I want you to notice, but her attitudes. She is living with fear that other people will reject her. And she comes off as an arrogant snob because she fears what other people will think of her if she doesn't meet their standards of lifestyle. Someone once quipped, "The richer your friends, the more they will cost you." How true.

Again, this is a case of a few bad examples spoiling the whole picture. But there's something else I'd like to point out to you. People who achieve true financial freedom do not have the attitudes this woman has. This woman is not free at all—she is in bondage to her money. Yes, she may have a lot of it, but she is not financially free. She is constantly worrying about what people think.

Also, she is a spender, not a producer. As I said before, there's a difference between having money and being wealthy. This woman demonstrates that difference through her attitude toward her money.

Image #3—The rich as pathetic personal failures. Many people in America are convinced that wealthy people are inwardly miserable, their lifestyles are horrible, their relationships are in wreckage, and they are spiritually empty. For years books have related the story about J.D. Rockefeller, one of the wealthiest men in the history of the world, who in his fifties purportedly developed a horrible ulcer. These books claimed he could not eat regular food because his stomach was ripped apart from stress and tension. But I found out after subsequent study and examination that the story was false. It was a myth. Rockefeller never had those stomach problems. In fact, he was a very healthy, happy man who lived well and productively into his nineties. Rockefeller was respected and loved by many people of his generation, but it seems that there are always people who are afraid to be rich or are jealous of those who are, and who convince themselves that all wealthy people are pathetic personal failures.

Image #4—Wealthy people as the heroes of society. There are still some who believe that most wealthy people are those who give money back to society, who build great empires, and who create jobs for millions of men and women. I believe that some rich people *are* criminals and outlaws, that some rich people *are* arrogant snobs, and that some rich people *do* live lives of pathetic personal failure. But I also believe that the majority of men and women who produce wealth in this country are heroes, and I say that they're to be commended as leaders of industry and commerce. We should be thankful for these men and women who produce wealth and for what they contribute to society.

Wealth and money are not synonymous with materialism. Editor-in-chief of *Leaders* magazine, Henry O. Dormann, has written, "The greatest joy is to see a man with ideals and dreams making wonders happen by using his wealth not as an instrument of vanity, but as a plaything of pride and joy." Wealth is a powerful and constructive force in our society. It is a worthy goal to be pursued and achieved.

Wealth is founded on a sane, realistic understanding of money. Materialism is a view of money and material things that has become warped, a kind of worship.

It's essential for you to understand the difference. For unless you can use the motivation of achieving goals, making money, and creating wealth, you will never become a productive and successful achiever in life. But if you can grasp this difference and overcome your fears of materialism, you can and you will accomplish great things!

Let me tell you something. We are living right now in a generation of booming opportunity. Do you realize that in 1859 there were only three millionaires in all of the United States: John Jacob Astor, Cornelius Vanderbilt, and August Bilmont? In 1987, for the first time in the history of America, there were one million millionaires! Don't tell me that America's great days are past. Don't tell me that the era of building great wealth is gone. I don't believe it. History doesn't prove it. Experience doesn't support it. We are living in a time of unprecedented opportunity. And I know you can listen to the gloom presented through the American media and you can be thoroughly misguided by those negative images of wealth.

I believe those images are completely untrue and unfair.

There are great opportunities in America, and they're within your reach! Don't let wrong thinking hold you back!

TWO
A SPIRITUAL PERSPECTIVE ON MATERIAL PROSPERITY

I talked to a man recently who said he feared that if he really gave himself to material goals, it would interfere with his spiritual goals.

I heard of a young couple who said that they wanted to be spiritual and didn't want to get preoccupied with material things. They said they were in great trouble financially. They couldn't pay their bills on time, were overextended, had abused credit cards, had taken installment loans, etc. But then the husband said something very interesting. He admitted that he couldn't even lead his family prayer times at home because all he could think about was their enormous load of debt and how to get out of it.

Let me tell you that when you're in that much debt, the most spiritual thing you can do is get your finances in order.

It is an absolutely spiritual thing to do. God made you, he made the world, and he made the material things in the world. We tend to relegate God to some mystical, spiritual, unreal world and never let him into our very real, material world and the practical things of our lives. In fact, God cares about your finances, your marriage, your sex life, your kids, and even your mortgage.

FOUR KEY TEACHINGS

Let me show you some of the things the Bible says about the material world.

First, God made it. It was his idea to begin with. It's not as if he created a spiritual world, and then the devil came and counterfeited it with this phony material world, tricking all of us. No. God actually made the material universe. That includes money.

Seven times in the first chapter of Genesis, God, in describing the creation of the world, says that the world he made is "very good." He gives it absolute approval seven times, and if you know anything about the subject of what is called Bible *numerology*—the study of the significance of numbers in the Bible—you know that the perfect number from the Jewish perspective in the Old Testament is seven. So God says seven times, the number of perfection, that the material world is very good.

Second, God tells you that you can be happy in his world. That's his intention. Deuteronomy 16:15 says, "The Lord your God will bless you in all your produce and in all the work of your hands, so that you surely rejoice" (NKJV). Isn't that tremendous! The word "produce" in the Hebrew means hard work, what you earn, what you contribute and produce. So you see, God's not a tyrant or an ugly, ferocious monster ready to choke your life out when you're having fun.

Third, God often uses material inducements to get his people to do something. Isn't that amazing— God uses material rewards as motivators! The Bible tells of how the Jewish people had been released from Egyptian slavery. The Egyptian army had just been obliterated trying to follow them and recapture them. So the Israelites are wandering around in this barren desert and they're having all these difficulties disciplining themselves to obey God. They're just getting in one fix after another. Well God gives them material promises. He says, "I'm going to give you a land that flows with milk and honey." That is an Old Testament symbol of great prosperity and financial freedom. He even goes so far as to say that their crops will be enormous. He will bless their cattle and give them silver and gold—money and prosperity. This is God speaking. God is bringing these people to obedience through material inducement.

Now maybe that makes you cringe. You know you ought to obey God because you love him, not because he rewards you if you do. But God knows us better than we do; he knows what incentives we need to obey him. God planted dreams of material things in the Israelites' heads to induce them to obey him and make it to the Promised Land.

It's ironic that if God did that today—and he really does through his Word—a lot of Christians would accuse him of materialism, because he is using material things to work in us.

Now I'm not saying that God stopped with material inducements. He certainly didn't, and God says that you ought to love the Lord your God with all your heart, and respond to him out of gratitude. But our God of wisdom does in fact use material things to reward us and motivate us. That says to me that the material world and prosperity are not evil in and of themselves.

Fourth, there are biblical examples of the positive influence of godly men who were rich. Abraham in the Old Testament was very rich. Genesis 13:2 says he was extremely rich. The word "rich" in Hebrew means this guy was mega-wealthy. He was on top. He may have been the wealthiest man of his generation. Back then there were several pagan, barbarian kings who did not obey or worship the true God. They went to Abraham for counsel. And God gave them godly counsel through Abraham.

Here's my point. The pagan kings did not go to Abraham because he was godly. They went to talk to Abraham because he was rich, and Abraham used the influence of his wealth to tell them about God. Now I believe that's a powerful challenge to Christians in this generation. If you'll get up and start achieving, if you'll do something financially to improve your life, if you get in a better position of influence in your community, and if you love God while you're doing it, then God will use your prosperity as a great reflection of himself. You will then have great spiritual influence over men and women who then will respect you and listen to you. People respect success. They are challenged by it and listen to it. God wants you in that position of influence.

I'm not saying that money alone is the influence. To give people godly counsel you must live a godly life and lead a great prayer life. You can only reach people spiritually on a spiritual level. But your achievement and your success can be a tremendous invitation to men and women to come and listen to you when you tell them about Jesus Christ.

TWO MISUNDERSTANDINGS

There are two verses in the New Testament that give people fits when it comes to money. They are grossly misunderstood. In fact one of them is probably the most consistently misquoted verse in all the Bible. You've probably heard it quoted like this: "Money is the root of all evil." That is the most misquoted verse in all the Bible. The verse does not say that money is the root of all evil. The verse actually says, "A love of money is a root of all kinds of evil."

First of all, the verse says it is "*a* love of money,"

not just "*the* love of money." The Greek grammar here implies an unbalanced love. It's an unusual love and devotion to money. A out-of-balance belief it they will meet all your needs.

The word "root" here is a key. It is a specific Greek word that technically means "shoot." I don't know if you grew up on a farm and know anything about gardens, but the difference between a root and a shoot is that a root is beneath the ground and a shoot is above the ground. A shoot is something that is the result of what you're growing. It is the stalk of the corn, the top of the carrot. The root is beneath, providing the nourishment to the shoot. So, a love of money is a "shoot" of all kinds of evil.

In this passage, Paul is counseling Timothy on how to handle a group of ungodly teachers. Men whose lives were constantly producing evil shoots. Their roots were evil, so they were having evil shoots. One of their evil shoots was that they had a wrong love of money. They were greedy and they cheated. So what the verse here is saying is this: "Timothy, you know all of these evil men—look at them, you can see them. All these men love money and they have a wrong, unbalanced love of money, and it's producing all these shoots that are growing out of their life. They've got all kinds of un- balanced, undisciplined results pouring out of their lives. So I want to warn you, Timothy, that that kind of unbalanced love of money is a root of all kinds of evil. It produces shoots of all kinds of other evils. Steer clear of it, don't have anything to do with it. That's not for you."

Now I want to ask you honestly. The people that use this verse to beat you over the head when you're trying to be an achiever—do you think they understand what it really means, or are they just quoting something they've heard from somebody else to try to intimidate you and keep you from being a winner and a success? No, most people don't understand this verse at all.

Now the other problem verse is Matthew 19:24: "It is easier for a camel to go through the eye of a needle than a rich man to enter the kingdom of God" (NKJV). Now what does that actually mean? Is Jesus saying that if you are rich you can't be saved? That doesn't quite add up according to some of the other things we know from the Bible. For one thing, some of Jesus' followers were very rich. Joseph of Aramathea was very rich. Nicodemus was a rich man who came to Jesus. And some of Jesus' followers were wealthy enough to give him gifts such as expensive perfume.

Let me explain what that verse really means. In Bible times, at night in the walled cities they shut the gates and locked them, usually after nine P.M. This was for security and protection. Nobody could go in or get out. But there was a small gate called a needle gate, and that was the eye of the needle that you could get through cautiously but with difficulty. And also there were certain areas in the city that were called needle streets or needle corners that were so small and so tight they were called the eyes of needles. Camels, which are big, ungainly creatures, to get through that needle gate or to get through that needle corner or needle street, would have to kneel down on their camel knees, often having to be removed of their burdens, and have to work their way through that gate carefully. I believe what Jesus is trying to teach here is a lesson in humility, a lesson on balance. He's saying it may be more difficult, though not impossible, for a rich man to be saved. Wealthy men and women may have their lives out of balance, perhaps becoming overdependent on material things, or needing them for self-image, or using them for status, and they may find it difficult to see past their material wealth and accept Jesus Christ into their lives. It is a question of humility and balance.

So you see, these verses and others like them are so confused and frequently misquoted. They're not prohibiting you from succeeding for God or achieving for Jesus Christ.

THE PRINCIPLE OF REMEMBERING GOD

Do you know what happened to the Israelites? They forgot the promises and provisions of God and wound up wandering in the desert for forty years. Here's how the Bible describes it in Deuteronomy 8: "Every commandment which I command you today you must be careful to observe, that you may live and multiply, and go in and possess the land of which the Lord swore to your fathers. And you shall remember that the Lord your God led you all the way these forty years in the wilderness, to humble you and test you, to know what was in your heart, whether you would keep His commandments or not. So He humbled you, allowed you to hunger, and fed you with manna which you did not know nor did your fathers know, that He might make you know that man shall not live by bread alone; but man lives by every word that proceeds from the mouth of the Lord. Your garments did not wear out on you, nor did your foot swell these forty years. So you should know in your heart that as a man chastens his son, so the Lord your God chastens you. Therefore you shall keep the commandments of the Lord your God, to walk in His ways and to fear Him. "

But here's where it gets really good—here's what God wanted to teach these people. Here's why they needed to be disciplined and learn his lesson. "For the Lord your God is bringing you into a good land, a land of brooks of water, of fountains and springs, that flow out of valleys and hills; a land of wheat and barley, of vines and fig trees and pomegranates, a land of olive oil and honey; a land in which you will eat bread without scarcity, in which you will lack nothing; a land whose stones are iron and out of whose hills you can dig copper. When you have eaten and are full, then you shall bless the Lord your God for the good land which He has given you."

Now, there is a balance, and here it is in verse 11: "Beware that you do not forget the Lord your God by not keeping His commandments, His judgments, and His statutes which I command you today, lest—when you have eaten and are full, and have built beautiful houses and dwell in them; and when your herds and your flocks multiply, and your silver and your gold are multiplied, and all that you have is multiplied; when your heart is lifted up, and you forget the Lord your God who brought you out of the land of Egypt, from the house of bondage; who led you through that great and terrible wilderness."

Now do you see the key principle here? "You shall remember the Lord your God." Verse 18 explains it clearly: "You shall remember the Lord your God, for it is He who gives you power to get wealth, that He may establish His covenant which He swore to your fathers, as it is this day."

Do you understand why this is so exciting for you and me today? Because the New Testament teaches in the book of Romans that when you come to know Jesus Christ you are an heir to the promises of Abraham. You complete the Jewish promises in the Old Testament. It's wonderful. It is the mercy and grace of God, so these promises apply to you as well. What I'm saying is this—God's purpose for you is abundance. It's success, prosperity.

Now, you have to work hard. God didn't just drop the Promised Land into the laps of the Israelites. If you read the book of Joshua, you learn that they had to fight their guts out to get that land. The Bible says in Deuteronomy 8:1 that you are to "go in and possess the land"—to win it. Possess means win it, work for it. But then it says not to forget God. You see there is a balance here. If you remember God, then you can succeed to the hilt without guilt.

GREEK VERSUS HEBREW THINKING

Now why is it, if the Bible is so clear on the principle of remembering God and the promise of God's prosperity, why are so many Christians confused by this? Why are so many churches poor? Why are missionaries having to spend so much time pressured by money to where they become ineffective overseas? Why do ministers have such low morale and such low salaries?

I believe it's because of the difference between Hebrew and Greek thinking in the modern church. Ron Ball, my co-author, explains it like this:

After the church had been functioning about 300 years, a great philosopher/teacher came along named Augustine. Augustine had a background of sexual looseness. He had fathered an illegitimate child, he lived with a woman to whom he was not married, and he was very weak in his morals. When he came to Jesus Christ, he was powerfully and profoundly changed. Augustine developed a wealth of great philosophical materials to lead the early church. He was one of the greatest intellectual geniuses that the human race has ever produced.

But Augustine made one serious, damaging mistake. He adopted not Hebrew but Greek thinking in two key areas: money and sex. He believed that the spirit was better than the flesh, the body.

Now there are different meanings for the world "flesh" in the New Testament. The Greek word for "flesh" is the Greek word "sarks." That's where you get the Egyptian term "sarcophagus" which means a body box, a flesh house, a body house. So the Greek word for flesh is really a neutral word, it's something God made and the flesh can be used for good or used for evil. But it doesn't have to be evil.

Now there is another word for "flesh" in the New Testament which means a fleshly, proud, arrogant, rebellious desire to go your own personal way—the way of the flesh. But flesh in the terms of the human body is not necessarily evil. God made it. Hebrew/Jewish thinking, which is what the Bible is based on, believes the body is good and right because God made it. Money and sex are good because God made them. Certainly there are spiritual laws that govern the use of sex and of the body, but Hebrew/Jewish thinking believes that the body is good.

The Greeks came along and said the spirit is what's better, and the body is corrupt. The Greeks began to put down sex and money and develop all of these abstract, intellectual philosophies that went against the essence of Hebrew/Jewish philosophies. And Augustine really swallowed this, maybe because of guilt over his past life, but he began to teach that it was so much better to exalt the spirit and put down the body. And all through Christian history, Augustan thought has dominated. I personally believe the devil has done that. It's created the dark, oppressive atmosphere of medieval monasteries where people deny their sexuality and repress themselves. It's created a twisted view of money, a thought that poverty is more pleasing to God than success. It's created a division of thought that's really not biblical. The biblical thought is that the body is good and should be used for God; sex is good and should be enjoyed for God within marriage; money is good and should be given back to God and its fruits should be enjoyed.

So, we're a victim of Greek thought. We must return to biblical, Hebrew thinking. We must return to a right Bible basis in our thoughts.

THE CHALLENGE
God wants you to build a successful life. I'm not saying that God has called you to become a multimillionaire, but God has called you to succeed in becoming all that you can become. You need to be the best you can be for Jesus Christ. God wants to use you to meet the needs of the world, and as he did in Bible times, he needs people like you to be successful and prosperous.

One of the real tragedies of our culture is the negative, low-class image people have of Christians. What the world sees—on Christian television, in the news, in churches— are Christians who are personal failures, hypocrites, and con men. The world cannot see past these images. In Washington D.C. the attitude toward conservative Christians is that we're on the lunatic fringe of life, that we're uneducated and poor, and that we're not successful in what we do. We've got a real image problem.

We've got to let people know that's not true. And through your godliness, linked with your achievements and success and your winning approach to life, you can destroy that myth, upgrade the Christian image around this country, and restore respectability to the work of a holy God. You need to become an exciting reflection of the greatness of a holy God. That's why I want you to succeed and do better.

I want to challenge you to begin now upgrading the image of Christians in your community, in your schools, in your work place, and even in your church. We've got to let people see that becoming a Christian doesn't mean that you become a failure, that you take a lackadaisical, sloppy approach to life.

Being a Christian demands that you perform at your best and that you realize your maximum potential for success. A noted seminary professor once said, "As a committed Christian who loves Jesus Christ, you ought to out-think, out-love, out-work, and out-produce the secular world, to earn their respect, gain their attention, so that they'll hear the truth about Jesus Christ from your lips in your life."

You've got to produce and perform so that you will have a platform from which to proclaim Jesus Christ, his principles, and his truth. Don't let misinformed Christians scare you into under-achieving for fear of the materialism label. You owe it to them and the world to be a better example, to gain more, to work more, to earn more.

THE BENEFIT

When you're a great achiever, not only will you improve the image and testimony of Christians in the world, but four things happen to your character that change you for the better.

1. You will grow in character. Your achievement means you have not been willing to live on the charity and sympathy of government and that you're not a person who lives on the sympathy of other people. You will develop self-respect, and you'll find that your family will respect you more and look up to you. You'll find yourself standing tall, holding your head up high. You will become more confident in making daily decisions, and you'll find that you handle crises more effectively and authoritatively. People will notice the change in your character.

2. You will find yourself becoming upwardly mobile because of other people's respect for you. Upward mobility is dependent on upward admiration. People need heroes, and constantly look for heroes in their lives. When you succeed and achieve, you become an example for other people, a hero to them. You become an example for the poor, for those that without that example might never change. George Gilder has written: "To accept lower class behavior, attitudes, and achievement is to betray the lower class and doom them to remain where they are." Your lifestyle becomes something that others will want to emulate—they will want to be successful as you are, and they will see your lifestyle as a magic formula for success.

Let me quickly point out that this respect for successful people is not the same as coveting what they have. Coveting is wrong; it is the desire to possess what someone else possesses. What we're talking about is a desire to *be*, to be what another person has become.

Achievement then is more than just something you do for yourself; you have to become more than you are so you can inspire people to become more than they are. You have to be better to give a model for people to become better. A society only improves itself by upward inspiration, motivation, and encouragement. It's vital that you continue to succeed as an example.

3. You become a strength for your family. You bring them security, protect them from pressure, provide stability. By removing unnecessary financial pressures, you take away unnecessary tension and worry, and your family can then develop in an atmosphere of good mental health, emotional balance, and spiritual growth.

One word of caution: some pressure is good. It motivates you to overcome. You need to teach your children how to handle it, to expect some of it in life. A friend of mine said to me recently, "The only people I have trouble with are the children of wealthy men and women, kids who never had to earn a dime. They don't know how to keep it. They run through it like water. They have pathetic attitudes about handling money and managing their accounts. I find that the sons and daughters who have been forced to work with their parents, who have had to earn it and learn the value of labor, are much more responsible." So while you want to provide for your family and remove unnecessary financial worries, it's still important for your children to learn the value of money and the techniques for managing it.

That said, you will find that as a financial achiever, your family life will improve because there will be less tension and frustration about money.

4. *You will find that achievement breeds manhood in men.* The primary crisis of this generation is a crisis of masculine identity. Men desperately need to know who they are. They need to know their role of leadership again in modern American life under God. The Bureau of the Census says, "The sharp rise in divorce and separation in this country is in direction proportion to the number of women taking on full-time work responsibilities outside the home." Families are being pulled apart.

Let me quote George Gilder again: "Families are destroyed when a man no longer feels manly in his own home." When a man succeeds and builds a dream, that man feels manly. He has performed. A man fulfills his sexual identity of manliness by performance, by productivity. When a man produces and provides for his family, it breeds manhood in him as a man and strengthens his role of leadership and respect in his family.

So what are you going to do about your life? I want you to make a commitment right now. I want you to make a commitment with all your heart. Understanding what we've seen about materialism and achievement and success, I want you to do one thing. You're going to surrender to Jesus Christ and with his power and help, you're going to succeed to the hilt without guilt. You're going to achieve without shame. You're going to accomplish without any anxiety. All for a great and glorious God, whom we love and whom we want to successfully project to the rest of the world.

THREE
ELEVEN REASONS
TO BE RICH

It's one thing to overcome the negative attitudes, cultural and spiritual, that people have toward being prosperous and successful. It's another thing to focus on the positive benefits of financial achievement and actively desire to achieve more in life. Surprisingly, many people need encouragement to pursue financial success!

I want to give you eleven reasons to be rich. I want you to get excited about what financial prosperity can mean for you!

Reason #1. To provide freedom and independence. Thomas Jefferson, considered one of our greatest presidents, said, "I can give you the definition of success in two words. Success equals freedom and independence." Lewis Lapham, the editor of *Harper's Magazine*, has a great statement on this point. He writes, "There is a difference between the people who earn things and the people who fear the owners of things." Many people are full of anxiety because they lack money. They don't have the power of choices and options.

I heard recently of a successful man who decided on the spur of the moment to take a vacation. He said, "I'm going to the Virgin Islands. I'll rent a boat and sail around for a week. I'd rather go in the winter cause it's nice and warm down there. It'll take me a couple of weeks to rearrange my schedule, but then I can take a week and do it." He had the power of choice, the power of options. He has earned it through many years of hard work and building wealth.

Before I started my own business back in 1964, I worked for a boss. Through the job requirements and my level of pay, my boss "told" me what time to get up in the morning, when to go to work, when I had to be in bed at night, how far I could go on my weekend off, what kind of vacation I could afford, where I could live, how many kids we could afford to have, and whom I could associate with. And then if I did something he didn't like, he could fire me. I was a slave. Many people who work for a boss think they have financial freedom, but only when you can name your own hours, set your own salary, and have the freedom to afford the level of life you want are you really free.

Many people don't realize how "unfree" they really are until they become financially prosperous and independent. Success, as Thomas Jefferson said, is freedom and independence.

Reason #2. To give you release from the petty problems of life. The tyranny of the little stuff. Let me give you a good example. For most people there's nothing more stressful than a car problem. But If I am driving back from a meeting and I'm three miles from home and my car breaks down—that's not a problem for me. I have options because I have money. I can hire a tow truck. I can pay for someone to fix my car. I can even buy another car. It's not a problem for me. It's just a minor inconvenience.

Not every problem in life, of course, can be solved by money. Illness, accident, and tragedy are things in God's hands. But many things *can* be solved by money, and don't have to be stressful parts of life.

If you're rich enough, you don't have to worry about all of the trivial problems of life that are so time consuming. You can concentrate on bigger issues. You can hire out the little things that need to be done, so you can have time to do the things you want to pour your heart into.

Reason #3. To build the character of self-respect and personal achievement. I was watching the Broadway play, *A Chorus Line.* This is a story of aspiring actors and actresses who want to make it big on Broadway. In the play, one of the women says, "All of the work will be worth it. All the late nights will pay off. All the sacrifice will be enough if I can just make it to the point where every morning I can get out of bed, look in the mirror, and be thankful that the person in the mirror is me."

You can be proud of your accomplishments. Yes,

the Bible does warn of a form of pride that will kill you. There's a pride that goes before a fall. There's an arrogant egotism that will wreck your life and destroy your success. But I'm talking of legitimate self-respect in personal accomplishment. Be proud of yourself and your achievements.

Reason #4. So you can live your life without financial fear. So many people live in continual fear. Lewis Lapham once said, "I always encounter men and women who are frustrated financially. Their attitude is if only they could quit the jobs they loathe. If only they could quit pandering to the whims of the company chairman or the union boss or the managing editor or the director of sales. If only they didn't have to keep up appearances. If only they didn't have to say what they didn't mean. If only they didn't have to lie to themselves and lie to their children. If only they didn't feel so small in the presence of money."

Perhaps you know what it's like to be settling in to your favorite chair at home at eight in the evening, and the phone rings, and you're afraid to answer it because it might be a bill collector. You know the feeling of not wanting to open your mail because you're afraid of the past-due notices you'll find. I think one of the greatest reasons to be rich is that it makes it possible for you to live without that kind of financial fear.

Reason #5. So you can live life in control. Of course, total control belongs only to God. But we can achieve limited control over our lives. One of the great things in my life is that I can pay every bill when it comes in. I've got control over that. In the past, if I left for a trip for two weeks, I used to have to wait and pay bills when I got back, but now whatever bill comes in, I can pay it the same day. I've got a limited control over that.

Reason #6. To give to others who need and deserve it. You can support causes you believe in. You can't do it if you don't have the cash flow to handle it. There are great causes that change the lives of men and women all over the world. And giving offers you the opportunity to help people in trouble who deserve help.

Now, I believe that the Bible always makes a distinction between the poor and the deserving poor. The deserving poor are those who can't help it, who would work and earn it if they could. But the poor are those who are poor because of laziness and lack of character, because they violated God's principles of wealth and success. Generally speaking, the Bible encourages you to help the deserving poor. Giving is a great reason to be rich.

Reason #7. To set a powerful personal example. I mean the example you set for your children, for people beneath you. There are people beneath you in achievement, not in value or worth, but they are beneath you socially and economically. They've not done what you've done, and your example for them gives them hope. You pull them up every time you succeed. You inspire them to win and accumulate and succeed.

In this way you can be a great example for your children. You need to train them how to manage money, how to make money serve them, and how to save and spend it.

Reason #8. To be an influence and a power for good in the world. Being an example is part of it, but concentrate on being an influence. Learn to be a moral champion. We are in a generation where we worship idols of entertainment, and many of these idols abuse their power of influence. If you make enough money, you can be a moral champion. Your money will give you a platform from which to proclaim what you believe. It will give you a stage of influence from which to broadcast what you believe is right.

Reason #9. Because you owe it to society to build and produce. This is a very 19th-century idea, one we've misplaced during the 20th century. You owe it to society to build and to give back some of what you've gained.

In fact, the Bible teaches that it is right for you to meet people's and society's needs. Just as God loves people, so should we love people by contributing our products or our services to others in the best possible way. When you meet the needs of people, that's part of God's love for them. If you sell somebody toothpaste and it protects their teeth and the teeth of their children, you've done something that pleases God. If you sell them vitamins that improve their health, you've helped meet their needs. You owe it to give back to others what God has provided for you.

Work in the Bible is glorified and dignified and good. Now, I know that some people have the idea that work is not spiritual. Some seem to think that preaching or praying or giving money to the church is spiritual, but our daily jobs have no spiritual value. But listen, all work, when it's honest and will meet somebody's need, is good. Say you work at an insurance claims department. You have dozens of claims coming across your desk every day, the work is tedious, and you become sloppy. But at the other end of that paper-work, hundreds of miles away in a small town, there's a mother who is trying to collect a death benefit so she can put food on the table for her three preschool children. And she's weeping and praying to God about her money. Meanwhile you sit there in that claims office, working slow and sloppy.

Your job, if you do it right and efficiently, is going to meet the needs of somebody God cares about. But if you do it carelessly and lethargically, some-one may be affected by your lack of discipline, desire, and commitment.

You owe it to society to be a giver and a builder.

Reason #10. Dignity and security in your old age. This is a really important reason to be rich, yet too many people fail to give it much thought.

I read a story of a man in a hospital in the Midwest. He was in his seventies and had been debilitated by a crippling illness. He was dis-couraged, not so much from his illness but from his inability to pay for the medical services he required. He also felt that his long stay in the hospital had dehumanized him. What he actually claimed was that, because he didn't have much money and was in a semiprivate room, his human dignity had been damaged. The way he was treated made him feel less than a person. His inability to afford better treatment made him dependent on the hospital and restricted his freedom to overcome the dehumanization of his situation.

If you're rich, when you get to your old age and you're sick, you can hire private nurses and private doctors. You can even buy a hospital if you're rich enough. You can be guaranteed dignity and security.

Reason #11. To glorify God. The Puritans taught it. Benjamin Franklin taught it. Russell Conwell taught it. Charles Spurgeon taught it. Cotton Mather taught it. They all taught that one of the great reasons to be rich is to glorify God, and I believe you glorify God through his Son, Jesus Christ.

Listen, God is a God of work. The whole creation is an expression of the work of God. If you still don't think that's true, listen to Psalm 104:10-28 (NKJV):

> *He placed springs in the valleys, and streams that gush from the mountains. They give water for all the animals to drink. There the wild donkeys quench their thirst, and the birds nest beside the streams and sing among the branches of the trees. He sends rain upon the mountains and fills the earth with fruit. The tender grass grows up at his command to feed the cattle, and there are fruit trees, vegetables*

and grain for man to cultivate, and wine to make him glad, and olive oil as lotion for his skin, and bread to give him strength. The Lord planted the cedars of Lebanon. They are tall and flourishing. There the birds make their nests, the storks in the firs. High in the mountains are pastures for the wild goats, and rock-badgers burrow in among the rocks and find protection there. He assigned the moon to mark the months, and the sun to mark the days. He sends the night and darkness, when all the forest folk come out. Then the young lions roar for their food, but they are dependent on the Lord. At dawn they slink back into their dens to rest, and men go off to work until the evening shadows fall again. O Lord, what a variety you have made! And in wisdom you have made them all! The earth is full of your riches. There before me lies the mighty ocean, teeming with life of every kind, both great and small. And look! See the ships! And over there, the whale you made to play in the sea. Every one of these depends on you to give them daily food. You supply it, and they gather it. You open wide your hand to feed them and they are satisfied with all your bountiful provision.

That's a God who loves work and is producing wealth. And look at the unbelievable wealth God has created! Listen, God himself works, and he works successfully. And likewise you glorify God through good work that produces results and rewards.

I'm not saying that God guarantees that everyone will become a millionaire. That's not what the Bible teaches. I believe the principles of the Bible indicate that it is God who gives the power to create wealth, and when you succeed to the maximum of your ability to make your best for God, you glorify him.

I want you to realize from these reasons to be rich that you don't have to be embarrassed by your accomplishments through hard work. You can enjoy success and influence and know that you've pleased God. I can't think of any other better way than to live with real financial security and to have all of these eleven things come true in your life.

FOUR
THE BASIC
BUILDING BLOCKS
OF ACHIEVEMENT

I hope you are now convinced that a successful life and financial prosperity are worthy and even spiritual goals to set for yourself. Now, there are certain things that are essential to building a lifestyle of achievement. One of the keys is to learn the habits of success. These are the building blocks of achievement. Let me explain them for you.

1. Belief. You will accomplish nothing without the belief that you can accomplish something. I don't mean just rah-rah, positive-thinking, motivational mental gymnastics, but I mean a deep, confident belief that you can achieve great things.

You need that kind of belief level. Unfortunately, there are the people who will try to tear down your belief, and sometimes these people are your own friends and family members. Maybe you intimidate them or threaten them. Your ambition for success probably shows up their excuses for failure. You're giving them an opportunity through your own inspiration and example to do something better with their life, which makes them uncomfortable and tense. But you can't give up your success just because they're choosing not to be a success. So you need a deep, powerful belief inside yourself. A belief that goes beyond self-assurance. A belief that you are *right.* That's the reason I've already spent the time that I have tackling this materialism myth problem, because otherwise you're inclined in this time and culture to think it's wrong to be a success. You need to believe that not only can you be an achiever and be successful and win at fulfilling your chosen dreams, but also that it's right to do so.

I want to give you an example of how this belief level works powerfully, and I want to use a racial example. Now, using a racial example doesn't make me a racist. But I want to make an illustration about the black community in this country. Statistically, blacks in this country are really having a tough time. The majority of unemployment is in the area of the black male population, and the majority of violent crimes in this country are committed by black men. That doesn't mean there is anything inherently wrong with black people, but because of the development of black culture in the last 150 years in this country there have developed some serious problems that need to be corrected.

But I don't believe welfare is the answer. Welfare

removes men from the economy as providers. One of the most devastating problems in black, inner-city culture is that men have been eliminated as providers. Through welfare, a woman with several children can be virtually independent of a man and can actually make more money than a man who struggles to find a decent job. So she eliminates the need for a man, she emasculates the men around her, and men grow up thinking that they aren't needed. Instead they become young bar-barians. They give themselves to drugs, crime, and sexual promiscuity; consequently they do not con-tribute to society. Now this can happen to whites just as easily as to blacks, and it does in some situations, but it just happens to be a bigger part of the black subculture at this point.

I believe one of the real problems of the black subculture is that many black people believe that they are inferior, and they believe that because they are convinced that they cannot make it without government support. They are convinced that the government has to intervene for them to have an equal chance with whites, and so their belief level, their confidence in themselves is tragi-cally, dangerously low.

Do you see what I'm saying? If for generations you have been told that you can't make it unless somebody does you a favor, then your belief in your own abilities is going to be weakened consid-erably. So I believe one of the worst things that has happened to black people in this nation has been the way certain ideas have been pounded into their thinking—that they cannot make it, that they are not capable of competing with a dominant white culture without massive, government-forced, affirmative action. That weakens black achievement. It is a devastating problem. I've heard one black leader himself say that affirmative action programs have devastated his people because it has removed their belief in themselves.

Now, you might say that you still think they need help. Well, Orientals coming to this country are not even able to speak English. They're not getting affirmative action help, yet they are outworking most Americans. They are becoming wealthy, and they're building businesses and dreams. They're working hard and making it on their own, with pride and self-respect. The story of Oriental immigrants in America shows up the depravity of our country's affirmative-action philosophy.

So you have to have a belief level. Because of these programs, the belief levels of many of our black citizens is very low. You have to believe that you can make it, and that your achievement doesn't come from somebody else doing you a favor.

2. Ownership. A Harvard University economist has written, "Spirit and motivation to succeed are best elicited by ownership." When you own something, you are proud of it, and you will work for it, build it, and improve it. Ownership does something to the human spirit. One of the basic principles of human freedom has always been private ownership. In the Bible, in the early pages of the book of Genesis, the principle of private ownership is prominent. People owned their own land and businesses.

I am convinced that Americans have built the dream of American prosperity on the basis of private business ownership. Every major corporation at one point was started by someone with a dream to be self-employed. Even the giant DuPont Corporation started on the banks of the Brandywine River in the 1700s when E.I. DuPont built a gunpowder works. He was self-employed and had a dream. Look what his dream turned into!

So, build your dream. I'm not telling you to quit your job or leave your particular position, but I am emphasizing that one of the building blocks of long-term achievement and success is the principle of ownership. Even a savings account can be ownership. You need to have something that you build on that is privately owned.

Let me offer another example—the Soviet economic system. Based on communism, the Soviet economy is a wreck. The Soviet Union cannot even feed their own people. Productivity is ridiculously low. Shortages of goods and services run rampant. Why? Because private ownership has been obliterated by the socialist structures of communism. People no longer have pride in their possessions, and therefore have no pride in themselves.

3. Team work. You need other people. I know you've heard people say, with a growl in their voice, "Oh, I made it on my own." "I pulled myself up by my own bootstraps." "I didn't need anybody else's help." "I did it myself." Well, that's just not true. Everybody needs help. People have helped me considerably, and consequently I want to help others. A business where everybody helps everybody is built on this principle. It's a biblical principle of support, love, and cooperation.

You know, the immigrant groups with the best records for financial success in this country are Jews and Orientals. Now, very significantly, and not by accident, they are also the same immigrant groups with the most highly developed sense of mutual cooperation. They're not cut-throat. They're not walking on other people or trying to jump on top of each other to get ahead.

Charles Swindoll, in his excellent book *Commitment to Excellence*, says he has interviewed too many American businessmen who, right at the moment they have a shot at a promotion, undergo a Jekyll-and-Hyde change. They become transformed in character, walking on other people, trying to manipulate others to get the promotion. They become uncharitable and unloving. This is one of the reasons American business is suffering right now. Japan outshines us in key areas because of its emphasis on teamwork.

So you need other people to help you. If people work for you, you should care about them and treat them as you want to be treated. I know that sounds familiar, doesn't it? Well, it's the Golden Rule. Dennis Waitley, in his book *Being the Best*, says that there is never a substitute for the classic

Golden Rule as spoken by Jesus Christ, that you have to treat even your employees the way you would want to be treated if you were an employee.

4. *Hard work.* There is no substitute for work. You don't get rich quick. You get rich slow. If your attitude is to make a quick buck and get rich quick, you will be terribly disillusioned. Sure, you may be able to make some quick money, but you won't have the principles and discipline to keep it. You won't maintain and sustain your success. According to a Harvard business study, the root of wealth is very simple. The root of wealth is work. Hard work. The lower classes in American history have had a tradition of succeeding by outworking the classes above them who have become complacent. The classes above them began to take it easy. That happened to the auto industry in this country. They began to take it easy, became cocky and proud, and they paid a price through foreign competition.

5. *Building for your family.* The majority of production in a capitalistic economy comes directly from married men who are working for their families, building security for their wives and children. That doesn't mean that wives or single men don't produce, but statistically the capitalistic economy is fueled by married men who are working for their families. Of the top business executives of the Fortune 500 companies of America, 83 percent of them are still married to their first wives. The people who become wealthy in this country are committed to their families.

George Gilder, a famous economist and contributor to the *Wall Street Journal,* says "To become wealthy, keep your family together. Work for them." So build for your family. Build for someone outside your own life. Build the dreams for your wife and your children. Build for their future and security. Build for their success.

6. Building for rewards. You must motivate yourself with rewards. It is a violation of human nature to think that you can work and not earn anything and be happy with that. That's why communism is a miserable failure. Communism would work if you could get rid of human nature. But communism violates reality. That's why it doesn't work. So you need to work for rewards. George Gilder has written, "The country will fail if the link between effort and reward is eroded." Socialism, which is essentially work without rewards, allows people to starve. The communist economy sags and fails, people lose self respect, and they are not rewarded.

Now remember, I said this earlier—rewards do not equal materialism. You are not a materialist because you reward yourself when you've earned something. You're not a materialist if your family has a better standard of living because you've worked for it. That's not materialism. That's achievement.

7. The building block of giving. One of the greatest rewards is being able to be a giver. The happiest people I know are givers. Rockefeller was the wealthiest man of his generation and became a billionaire when money meant even more than it means now.

Andrew Carnegie gave away more than 80 percent of his vast estate to causes in which he believed. He experienced the joy of giving. You want to be a giver if you're a Christian. The book of Malachi says that one of the principles of the Bible is tithing—giving back to God (the church) 10 percent of your income, 10 percent of what God has given to you. God does miracles when you tithe and give. You'll find that your income will not suffer. Some people are afraid to tithe because they think it's too much a chunk out of their paychecks. That's a groundless fear not supported by the Bible nor by experience of people who obey the Bible's principles. You never lose by tithing. If you selfishly horde your money by yourself, God will let you handle your own financial problems, and that's no fun at all. You should tithe and give because God says do it, because it brings greater prosperity, and because it brings deep, profound joy in your spirit. It's the right thing to do.

These are the building blocks of success. They bring the balance that is necessary for continued success and accomplishment. You need to incorporate them into your life and build your success on this strong foundation.

Part II
THE KEYS
TO
FINANCIAL
PROSPERITY

FIVE
THE DREAM PRINCIPLE

Dreaming is the fundamental fuel of my life. Dreaming increases my level of energy, helps me overcome obstacles, and creates a clear focus on my future. I know where I'm going because of the power of my dreams. You will never have financial freedom without a clear vision of where you are going. You need to be able to grasp what you really want. You need the power of the dream to work for you.

Ben Franklin once said, "Dead at age twenty-one. Buried at age sixty-five. The Average American." People die when they stop dreaming. Men without vision will perish. A lot of people are walking around dead and don't know it.

Couples date, get excited about each other, and have tremendous energy and motivation to see each other again and again, as often as possible. A guy can work twelve hours a day and still make time to see his girl. He makes time for that because it's his dream. In fact, it's probably the one thing that helps him get through his twelve-hour workday. But the story continues: the couple gets married. They settle down. The responsibilities of life begin to weigh them down and begin to dampen their dreams. They each stop dreaming, both feeling trapped. Eventually, they get divorced. She says he's not the man she married. She may be right—he stopped dreaming along the way.

Let me say something parenthetically right here. A lot of guys have been married twenty or thirty years and they refer to their wives as "the old lady." Let me tell you that my wife is not my old lady. She's my special girl, my sweetheart, the love of my life. She's a dream come true to me. My dream is still real and because of that our marriage is still vital and vibrant. But couples whose dreams have died are relationships that have died as well.

Achievement is built on dreams. A life without a dream is a life of failure and despair.

THE FOCUS OF YOUR FUTURE

I've noticed in recent months much controversy erupting in much of the conservative press about the subject of visualization. Some Christian books, for example, condemn the process of visualization, while motivational books and journals elevate it to great importance.

What exactly is visualization? It's a mental technique. You picture in vivid, clear terms what it is you really want. You create an intense picture of where you're going. And that picture is constantly in front of you. You visualize it, you feel it, you touch it, you taste it, you see it, you live it.

Now the controversy comes because there are some groups that say this is part of New Age thought and philosophy. They say that visualization is like black magic or witchcraft, and you ought not to picture things you want. They say the Bible says not to worship idols and this could become a mental idol.

I believe this is a serious misunderstanding of the visualization process. This is not related to New Age thought, although New Age seekers may use the same technique of visualization. But there's an unfortunate "guilt-by-association" here. It's as if you wanted to condemn automobiles because a mass murderer in California drove a car. You wouldn't sell your car because some evil person also drove a car. No. The same thing is true regarding the technique of visualization. It may be used by groups of people we don't agree with, but that doesn't make it wrong.

Visualization is simply a mental process, a technique to help you reach your goals. Visualization— dreaming—gives a focus to your future.

Now what is the difference, you might ask, between a dream and a fantasy? A dream is something you are willing to work for, to put the effort into producing. You are willing to do what it takes to make the dream come true. It is a mental goal. It is a future focus. A fantasy, however, is something you hope for, but you never work at. Something you hope will happen to you, but which you never put in the effort to make come true. Visualizing making a million by winning the lottery is a fantasy. Visualizing making a million by going into business for yourself is a dream. So a dream and a fantasy are very different. In order to have dream power released in your life—in order to have the energy of dreaming poured into your finances—you need a clear future focus.

Visualization techniques go a step further. Not only do you see your dream, but you imagine yourself experiencing it. You picture yourself in it, as being in the position that you want to be in.

I read of a man just recently who wanted to be elevated to a certain position in his organization. He was far from it. He did not have the education, the training, the seniority, the experience, or qualifications needed for this particular position. But he forced himself—disciplined himself—to picture himself in that position. He pictured himself dressing in a certain way, acting in a certain fashion, and vividly "imaged" himself being responded to by other people. The more he did this, the more he acted the part. He started playing the role. And in a real sense he actually helped himself become that person.

This works in another way. Do you ever notice that some people always seem to have the knack of making good deals in the things they buy? This is a form of visualization at work. A person sees a car that has a rusted body, but knows that mechanically it's sound. For a small investment, the car might be restored. This person pays a pittance for a car that to most people looks like a wreck. The buyer, however, sees it's potential and from the beginning has visualized the car restored, shiny and gleaming, and has even pictured himself driving it down the street.

Do you want to discover the potential in things? Do you want to discover the potential in yourself? Do you want financial freedom? If so, you have to start dreaming dreams. You must imagine yourself already experiencing them. This is a basic psychological principle. It is a fundamental truth of life. Even the Bible says what you imagine in your heart is what you will produce. The Bible says in the book of Proverbs that you should guard your affections and your inner heart above all else, because what you focus on in your affections, in your imagination, in your heart, will probably be what you produce in your life. If you are thinking continually about pornography and about lewd and improper acts with men and women, your "dream" may come true in a disastrous way. But if you're dreaming about positive, good relationships and events, you will find that wonderful things will happen to you.

Perhaps you're thinking about buying a home. You are imagining the home you will live in. You are walking up and down the stairs of this future home. You are looking at the carpeting and you know what color it is, and you are sitting in the chair in the living room, watching the fire sparkle and blaze and crackle in the fireplace. You can see it and smell the smoke from that fire. You see yourself in this dream, and you're proud of your accomplishment. Maybe you live in an apartment in a less desirable part of town right now, but you can see the fireplace and you can see the good neighborhood, and the quality school just down the street for your children. You can see all of it. You now have a future focus.

Your future focus empowers your life. It gives you energy to get out of the bed in the morning and work toward your dream. Sometimes you don't want to get up. But you get up anyway because of your dream. You want to achieve your dream, and that becomes a great motivator.

I always have dreams in the making. I have ten to twelve major goals that I am reaching for all of the time. And if I reach one goal, I replace it with another. I always have multiple dreams pulling me, energizing me, building me, strengthening me. I always have a clear future focus.

Dream power will make your future focus work too.

FUEL FOR THE FIGHT

I heard a mythical story once. Satan visited the earth. He was watching a particular man who was preaching about Jesus Christ. When Satan observed this, some demons appeared beside him and asked, "Should we do something to disrupt the service? Should we try to stop this man's ministry?" Satan laughed and replied, "No, you don't need to interfere with this man. He's almost ours. We've almost destroyed him already." His demons said, "But he's preaching the truth, telling people about the Bible and Jesus Christ. We must stop him." And Satan said, "Listen carefully to this man and catch the note of discouragement in his voice. This man is discouraged and depressed. I tell you he is almost ours because discouragement is killing him."

That's why dream power is so important in your life. You must overcome the crippling effects of mental discouragement. Let me tell you it will come. You will have times when your dreams seem so far in the future you may never reach them. At some point, discouragement will set in. It will seem as if your dreams are receding ahead of you and that you just can't catch up with them. It will then get harder to sacrifice, harder to drive the extra miles in your car, harder to work later at night. It will become more comfortable to lounge in front of the television, easier to forget your dreams, simpler to give up on your future and hope.

But your dream power can come to your rescue. Your dream power can rebuild your energy supply and be the fuel you need for the fight.

Believe me, financial freedom is a fight. I see books frequently titled *The Easy Way to Become a Millionaire* or *A Simple Formula for Total Financial Freedom,* and the more I see these titles, the more suspicious I become, because there is no easy way to do these things. There may be good ways, enjoyable ways, effective ways, but there are no *easy* ways. It takes work, commitment, discipline, faith, and effort to produce financial freedom.

So your dreams will fuel you for this fight in which you are engaged. Your dream power will give you the fuel and energy that you will feed on. You will learn not only to visualize your dreams, but you will feed on your dreams. These images in your mind will nourish your achievements.

I am now almost fifty years old, but my approach to life as a teenager was very similar to what it is right now. I had dreams as a young man and they were very specific. I married Birdie because I knew I could build my long-term dreams with her. I wanted to marry for life, and I knew she had a great capacity for loyalty and would stick with me through the fight. I wanted lots of kids to run the businesses I one day planned to have. All of these things I have today started way back then as dreams, visualizations of the future. In fact I started dreaming of owning my own company when I was just ten years old. I worked my way through school. I always had some kind of job, whether it was mowing lawns, selling newspapers, cleanup work for neighbors, working in a clothing or hardware store, doing construction jobs, or developing my own soda business. I always worked and always pictured someday that through hard work I would get my own company.

I have learned in my life that I never reach a dream without it being specific. The more specifically I can visualize it, the more real it becomes.

Now, let me sum this up in simple fashion.

1. You must have a dominate dream. You must

have a dream that is the major focus of your future. You must have a dream that represents what you really want.

2. *You must imagine yourself already living in the reality of that dream.* The dream fulfilled. Visualized.

3. *Dreams must be specific.* Detailed. You must know the taste of it, the smell of it, the feel of it. You know what you want exactly.

NEVER STOP DREAMING

You must never stop dreaming of what you want to accomplish. I believe God is honored and pleased when people are constantly improving. So you should have spiritual dreams of your relationship with God through Jesus Christ. You should have self-improvement dreams of your intellectual expansion through reading. You should have physical dreams of always improving your level of health and vitality. You should have family dreams of increasing the quality of your relationships. You should have dreams for your business and your finances. You should have dreams that will work for your life.

You see, dreaming should be a natural mechanism, an automatic response in your life. One of the saddest situations of human existence is the man or woman who has lost the power to dream, even the desire to dream. The man or woman with emptiness in his or her eyes. The dull look of resignation, of mediocrity, of going through the mechanical motions every day of getting up, going to work, coming home, watching television, paying the bills, waiting for the weekend. No energizing dreams. No great purposes. I tell you God did not intend men and women to spend their lives in wasted mediocrity. It's not what God intends for the human race that he created for greater things and purposes than just survival existence.

I've recently become aware of a fascinating book about the Civil War era and the leadership of Abraham Lincoln. Lincoln exercised strong, wise leadership, and his dream was the reunion of the country when the rebellious components of the nation would be brought back and the United States would again be one whole federal republic. Lincoln never swerved from this. The America we have today exists because of Lincoln's stubbornness and his dream for reunion. He never failed to pursue that dream.

Likewise every person who accomplishes anything significant in life does so with a dream. Every achiever has a specific idea of what he wants. Every winner has a specific idea of what he wants.

You need dream power. You need dreaming ability. Some of you have been discouraged, your hopes have been dashed, you have lived a pattern of broken disappointment, and you have never witnessed your dreams coming true. In that life of discouragement, you now feel that there is nothing much for you to hope for, and you need to have your dream ability reawakened. You need your dream power released. Believe me, it's not too late.

You can still dream. You may have been beaten down and shattered by negative circumstances, but you can still win. History is filled with thousands of examples of men and women who refused to give up their dream, who would let no one kill the dream within them. Because of that, because they fought the fight, they reached dreams which other people thought were impossible to attain.

Dream power. It will give focus to your future and fuel for the fight. The fuel that you will need if you are going to win your fight for financial freedom.

SIX
THE WORK PRINCIPLE

When you go to a local bookstore, you see numerous books on success. Every business section contains volumes on how to be wealthy, and many of these books offer shortcuts to success and financial freedom. I know you may buy a book like this, looking for a formula, an "ABC," "1-2-3" program that supposedly produces great success automatically. And, yes, there are certain formulas that are important, and there are certain outlines that you do need to follow.

But there is one very simple truth about success. *There is no success without very hard work.*

In the 19th century, success was under the umbrella of what is called "character-ethic" teaching. This means that in 19th century of this country, it was very clear that in order to be a success you had to exhibit certain traits. For example, G.A. Hintey, an English Victorian author, wrote eighty adventure stories for schoolboys. He was very popular, and he always had a motto for success in all of his stories:

"If a lad from the first makes up his mind to do three things: to work, to save, and to learn, he can rise in the world." So this was common teaching back then, that there was no substitute for hard work. It's still true today. The truth about success is you must work to produce it.

I read recently of a man who said somewhat humorously: "Isn't it strange that success is usually disguised as hard work." Now I know that some of you shy away from this. You want an easy way to make money. You want a quick shortcut to success. The truth is there is no shortcut. The truth is you have to work hard in order to be successful.

I know that insider-trading scandals in the last few years on Wall Street have popularized the idea that if you just cut the right deal, if you can put together the right syndicate, if you can maneuver yourself correctly, the money will pour into your pocket. And it's true that sometimes you can cheat and steal and temporarily achieve a measure of financial success. But that's not true success. Because really you are paying a huge price—the sacrifice of your character. You kill who you really are, and then you are eventually caught in your deception. Every person who follows criminal activity eventually pays a disastrous price for that wrong activity.

You want real success? You want financial well-being? There is no substitute for hard work.

How many of us fight laziness? I've got it in my own life. Frequently I would get up in the morning and think, "I don't want to go out. I don't want to be working. I want to be in bed." The bed is inviting. The covers are so comfortable. It's wonderful to be in bed. But I get up, get going, and get doing. I feel responsible to work for my dreams to come true.

You need to realize that there is no truth that you must learn more urgently than the truth that success comes from hard work. The formula for success is there are no other formulas. The shortcut to success is realizing there are no shortcuts. It is all a matter of having a dream, and then work, work, work. Every person who has ever built anything significant has done so with labor—with the fuel and the capital of hard work.

Recently I was reading the life story of J. Paul Getty. When he died, he was a billionaire—the wealthiest man in the world. But even as an older man J. Paul Getty worked hard. This was even after his fortune was made. He was committed to the principle of work.

All of truly successful men and women work hard. So you must get it into your head right now—in order to be successful and financially prosperous you must work hard. If you were expecting something else, a simple formula, put this book down and look elsewhere. But let me tell you that a simple formula won't work.

CHANGING YOUR ATTITUDE TOWARD WORK
If you're still reading, I will assume you are at least beginning to accept this idea that hard work is at the core of true success. Let me suggest a few

concepts about work that may change your attitude toward it.

1. The ability to work is a gift. What if you could not work? What if you were physically disabled? What if you didn't have the mental ability to produce good work? Or what if you were unable to get a job, or even a job at a lower level than where you currently are? Then you would realize what an incredible, extraordinary blessing work really is. We take for granted the ability to work, and because it's something most of us have to do, we begin to resent it. But if we would only consider the alternatives—unemployment, ill health, lower-level employment—we would come to appreciate the gift that work is, and even come to appreciate more the work we're currently employed to do.

2. Work is a financial asset. Hard work is the ability to transfer your labor into a financial or material reward that you can enjoy.

A few years ago a book was published entitled *Sweat Equity,* and it talked about businesses being built by young men and women all over America who didn't have much money. But they had "sweat equity," the monetary value of their labor. And they built their businesses by sweat equity.

In the mountain region of Kentucky, where my coauthor, Ron Ball, grew up, there are many businesses that have existed for years, in an isolated region without much outside capital. The reason these businesses remain strong and continue to grow over the years is because they are family businesses and all those involved in them work—

from the children to the grandchildren, aunts, uncles, and grandparents—everybody works.

So you have to put your labor into something, and isn't it great that you have something like your own labor to contribute? Nobody else really owns your labor—you own it. And you can give it and use it wherever you choose. You can put your labor wherever you want to put it.

It doesn't really matter what level of labor you're working at. Whether you're in a blue-collar job or a white-collar job, it still is a financial asset that can work for you. Sometimes the relative value of those categories of jobs can be deceiving. I like the quote by former Secretary of Health, Education, and Welfare, John Garner: "An excellent plumber is infinitely more valuable than an incompetent philosopher. The society which scorns excellence in plumbing because it is a humble activity and tolerates shoddiness in philosophy because it is an exalted activity will have neither good plumbing nor good philosophy; neither its pipes nor its theories will hold water."

3. *Work seems harder when it's less enjoyable.* A lot of people say how hard their work is. But they're working harder in their mind than in their body because they're not liking what they're doing. Henry Ward Beecher once said, "Work is not the curse, but drudgery is."

When you have a real love for your job, time doesn't matter. In fact, time flies, and you begin to want to work longer hours. You put in sixty to eighty hours a week and don't think twice about it because you enjoy it and you know you're going to be a success at it.

There is something else to be said here. Work is often as enjoyable as you make it. Real achievers often have to do jobs that they don't like. But they find ways of motivating themselves anyway. They choose to make work rewarding and enjoyable, and so it becomes exactly that.

4. *Many people work hard, but fail to work smart.* They'll do certain tasks themselves that they don't care for, when they have the power to delegate or reassign these tasks to others under them. It's a basic management principle, but it's amazing how many people don't follow it.

Sometimes people wind up doing tasks that don't really need to be done. If they had been a little smarter, they might have saved themselves a lot of effort. The story is told of a man who was driving on a lonely road one summer day. He saw a car with a flat tire pulled over on the shoulder of the road. A woman was standing next to the car and looking down in dismay at the flat tire. The man decided to pull over and play the Good Samaritan. He grew hot and sweaty and dirty in the hot sun as he changed the tire. The woman was watching him, and when he was finished, she said, "Be sure and let the jack down easily now, because my husband is sleeping in the back seat!" So work hard. But also work smart!

Some people are working in a job they don't like, but they don't take the initiative to get into a job they do like. It's not a matter of experience or education or training. Many achievers didn't have those things to start with either.

As a young man I didn't have much education. But I knew I had one thing going for me—I wasn't afraid of work. I truly believed no one could out-work me. And as I worked, and worked hard, I found I could rise to the top and realize my dreams even though I had little formal education in those areas. The truth is that for a lot of jobs employers look past the superficial issues of training and education and value and look for the qualities of diligence, hard work, common sense, and on the job smarts. Character means a lot these days. And training for most positions these days really oc-curs on-the-job anyway, not in classrooms.

A lot of people complain about their bosses. The typical discussion involves talk about how the boss is stupid or incompetent in one way or another. But what's wrong with this picture? These people are working for that boss; that boss is smart enough to have these people working for him.

Real achievers, you see, are people who work hard, but also work smart.

5. *Real achievers see work as play.* You make a living working eight to five; you make a fortune working after five. When someone starts thinking in terms of an eight-to-five job, they've already made their first mistake—they see work as some-thing they have to get over with, instead of as a tool for their future achievement and promotion. Executives in big corporations don't work forty hours a week—they work sixty, eighty hours a

week. There's a reason that they're executives.

I know that's hard. Some jobs are tedious. But that's one of the keys to success in your work. Some people play golf; some people play tennis; some people play work. The key is to convert your mind from seeing work as drudgery into seeing work as play. Look for the fun in it; if there isn't any—create some. Get your mind off what you don't like and concentrate on what you do like. If you start changing your thinking, you'll find out that instead of hating your job, you'll start loving it.

6. Work is more enjoyable when you can be proud of what you do. Work at doing a better job. Quality and performance can be great rewards and great motivators.

There's a lot of emphasis today on companies and corporations developing incentive programs and motivational techniques to help employees produce more. These sometimes fill a need, but it amazes me that so many employees come to expect their company to motivate them to do good work. I was brought up to believe that work was pride in performance, and that it was your job, as a worker, an employee, to do your best. You don't slough off at work and show off on the handball court.

You'll become an achiever if you don't need to depend on company motivation techniques to become excellent in your work. You'll be successful if you strive for excellence on your own. And you'll discover that your job becomes more meaningful and more enjoyable if you simply try to do a little more and do a little better each time.

SEVEN
THE PERSEVERANCE PRINCIPLE

You've heard of the Lone Ranger of television fame, played by Clayton Moore, a cowboy hero with his Indian sidekick, Tonto, and his famous horse, Silver.

That's the Lone Ranger, but I am the *Long* Ranger. I'm committed to the long haul. I am in it to win it forever. A long ranger is one who understands one of the most important principles of success—the necessity of perseverance, or more simply, good ol' "stick-to-it-iveness."

A long ranger is characterzed by five things.

First, a long ranger is a long-termer. Life lasts from now till the day a long ranger dies. That's a long time. A long ranger realizes he has a lifetime to build his success.

Many people get into business and after three or six months see that nothing much has happened. So then they get out. Yet the average person spends four years going to college, and most college grads don't expect their education to really start working for them until many years after that. We seem to expect education to take a long time, but we fail to realize that business also takes a long time. When you start a business, the first four or five years are going to be an education process— just like going to college.

A story is told about the American violinist, Fritz Kreisler. After he had finished a concert and had gone backstage, Kreisler heard someone say, "I'd give my life to play as you do!" He turned and looked at the lady and replied, "Madam, I did."

Most people don't give themselves four or five years, much less a lifetime, to accomplish something. They get discouraged after six months. You have to give yourself ample time to succeed. You need to be a long ranger and hang in there, long enough and strong enough to succeed.

Second, a long ranger copes with rejection. Rejection is a common challenge to those who are building success. Dr. Thomas J. Stanley, president of the Affluent Marketing Institute of Atlanta, is an expert on American millionaires. He has spent years studying their habits, lifestyles, and the ways in which they produce. He says, "One thing all of them have in common—they have to overcome rejection."

Thomas Peters is probably the best-known management consultant in the world, coauthor of the bestselling books *In Search of Excellence* and *Thriving on Chaos*, a man who has had enormous impact on managerial thinking all over the world through the decade of the eighties. Peters said recently, "Opposition, criticism, and rejection are not prerequisites for success. They are not requirements for success. However, I have never studied a great' success who did not have to overcome great amounts of opposition, criticism, and rejection."

Money Magazine reports that in order to be a successful telephone solicitation stockbroker in New York you have to make at least 200 calls a day because so many of the calls end up with rejections.

Rejection is a part of the process of success. Learn to handle it and triumph over it. Defeat isn't bitter, if you don't swallow it.

Third, a long ranger exhibits staying power. Donald Trump said recently that the reason he was able to make great money out of some of his properties was because he had staying power. He had enough money to stick with it when others could not hold out.

Several years ago Ron Ball dabbled in the stock market. He got to a point where he really needed the money he had invested. So he sold the stocks and got his money back. He didn't lose any money. Now this sounds like a happy ending to a good story. However, three months later, the stock he had owned tripled in value. Ron, in that case, didn't have staying power, and as a result he lost out on a tidy profit.

I sometimes buy properties that I will keep for ten, fifteen, twenty years. Sometimes I keep them longer than that in order to make them as profitable as possible. My pattern is to go into an area, eye property, see something potentially valuable, buy it at a low price because it's yet undeveloped, and hold on to it long enough to see the investment grow in value. Being a long ranger, I often make many, many times my initial investment.

Fourth, a long ranger outlasts challenges. Every enterprise faces challenges. Do not fall under the illusion that as you become more successful your problems will go away. Rather, the more successful you become, the more problems you will have. They will be different. Sometimes even bigger. But they will be there. If your success becomes a large success, then you will have large problems to go with it. Don't be discouraged. Don't feel down. It's just a fact of life.

Someone has said, "The door to the room of success swings on the hinges of opposition." If you're a long ranger, you will outlast the challenges you face. And you will still be around when the challenges have faded and gone.

Fifth, a long ranger shows love and patience toward other people. Now maybe you don't see this as being a part of the principle of perseverance, but I do. In your quest for success, the greatest challenges you face will come from other people. Other people not only will oppose you, but they will try your patience. Let me tell you, to be a success you have to work—and love—the people around you.

So being a long ranger requires that you exhibit

love toward people, even sometimes when you don't want to. Many years ago I worked with an organization that served the elderly. I was holding meetings in this particular couple's home. They were about my parent's age. Every night their friends would come for these meetings. I noticed that they hugged and kissed each other in friendship. Well, I never grew up hugging and kissing in my family. I loved my parents, but I didn't tell them I loved them. So the experience of hugging and kissing in this situation was uncomfortable for me to be around.

After one meeting, I got into my car, and I satrted to cry. It was like leaving a second home. I was so moved by the show of love that these people had for each other. I realized that day that I was the leader of this group. They had accepted me as part of their group. I had to accept their show of love and return it back to them. I realized I needed to let them know—to show them—that I loved them just as they loved me.

This was difficult for me because it simply wasn't the way I had grown up. But I knew it was something I had to do. I had to tell them and show them that I loved them too. And that's what I did.

Don't get the idea that being a success means that you need to be a hard-nosed businessperson who every morning climbs into a hard shell of cold, calculating decision-making. Sure, you need to be shrewd, but a truly successful person values the people around him and doesn't let his success change him into a non-person.

So, are you a long ranger? There is great power in being a perseverer, one who waits patiently on decisions, investments, and people. Being a long ranger will work for you and lead you to achieve more, much more, than those who conduct themselves rashly and impatiently.

EIGHT
THE INVESTMENT PRINCIPLE

J. Paul Getty once wrote, "I have an allergy. It's been with me since I was small. I am allergic to spending money."

In fact, J. Paul Getty's father, George Getty, on one occasion in Bartlesville, Oklahoma, in 1905, was going to see a piece of land that he was considering buying lease on for the purpose of oil excavation and exploration. He asked a man to give him a ride. It was a long way—several hours round trip, on dusty, dirt roads by horse and buggy. When he returned to the town of Bartlesville, he thanked his friend for taking him but offered him no money at all for the journey. The man drove away, but stopped a short time later to jot in his diary, "I went with George Getty today to look at some land. He paid me nothing. He offered me no money. He thanked me, but there was no money. I believe some day he will be a rich man."

I'm not saying Getty was right or wrong in not

offering his friend some money for having taken him out to see the land. There is also a great principle of generosity that should work in a man's life. But the story illustrates strongly the principle of not spending money needlessly.

The investment principle begins simply with a question: to spend or not to spend? Do you want to spend your money or not? Do you want to spend it on things that will not last, or do you want to invest it on something that will? *The Richest Man in Babylon*, the well-known book on money management, teaches simply that if you do not spend your money, if you save it and invest it, you will build a strong financial foundation for your future.

I believe there are four key parts to the investment principle.

First, you must answer the question: Are you going to be an investor or a spender? Are you looking for ways to quickly spend your money or are you looking for ways to invest your money so it will begin to work for you? You will never become rich, you will never be a great financial success, you will never reach the heights of financial security and freedom unless you are an investor. It is a basic principle. There has never been a person who has achieved great success or accumulated great wealth that achieved it without investment.

Second, you must learn to avoid an all-consuming lifestyle. This is the hardest part of the investment principle for most people. What this means is that you cannot be someone who is so dominated by your immediate desires that you burn up all your income purchasing luxury items. You don't want to pour your money into lifestyle. Remember—you are living by the investment principle. If you are committed to an all-consuming lifestyle, you will consume your capital before you can invest it. You will be part of the consumer generation. What you are really trying to do is build a foundation for future freedom. That's investment. You have to think in the long term.

Third, the investment principle works one step at a time. It goes hand in hand with being a long ranger. When you invest in something, you don't do it for a quick, easy return. Your biggest returns are down the road. You must learn to think with a long-ranger perspective. The investment principle and the long ranger principle should shake hands in your life.

Fourth, you must invest in yourself. In my book, *Millionaire Mentality* I tell the story of Ewing Kauffman, founder and principal stockholder of Marion Laboratories in Kansas City, Missouri. His many investments include ownership of the Kansas City Royals, but Kauffman considers the dollars that he plowed back into himself when he founded Marion Laboratories his best investment.

Kauffman had been a pharmaceutical salesman. Back then the major pharmaceutical laboratories supplied drugs in containers of 500 to 1,000 each. Kauffman saw the possibilities of pre-measured containers of 100 tablets, making it unnecessary for the druggist to count tablets when filling the prescription.

Kauffman and his wife, with a couple of friends, began in the basement of their home, buying drugs in large containers and transferring them to bottles of 100 tablets each. It was the beginning of Marion Labs. The funds generated by the small surcharge on the smaller packages was reinvested. It ultimately made Mr. Kauffman one of the wealthiest men in America.

Sometimes people come to me asking my advice on where they should invest their money, and the answer is staring me in the face—it's the people themselves! On a recent trip to Milwaukee, I chatted with a young black woman, obviously well-educated, who was driving the taxi from the airport to my hotel. As we continued our discussion, I learned she had a degree as a paralegal, but she had found she could make more money driving a cab. She owned the taxi in which we were riding, as well as three others for which she had hired drivers. She mentioned that she had been able to save considerably from her profits and sought my advice on investing her money. "Are you operating all the taxis you can efficiently operate?" I asked. "No," she replied. "I think I could still make money with several more taxis." "Then invest the money in the thing which has made money for you," I told her. "You should make outside investments only when you have reached the point of diminishing returns investing in yourself."

That's a difficult lesson for us to learn. We think

in terms of investing, meaning that we have to give our money to someone else, but the best investment you can ever make is in yourself. Only when you have reached the point where you can no longer profitably invest in your own vehicle (job or company) should you seek to invest in others.

Mr. Hwang was a poor Korean immigrant when he arrived in the United States in the 1960s. He founded his company, Televideo, in 1976. The net worth from his company ownership alone is estimated at $769 million. Not a bad return for a seven-year investment in oneself.

People ask me if they shouldn't invest in stocks. Well, I say the times when stock investment makes the most sense is when you have the power to influence the stock yourself.

Let me remind you that a stock quite simply is a certificate representing a percentage of ownership in a company and stated as a number of shares. The percentage of ownership obviously depends upon the number of shares outstanding. Ten shares in a company with only 100 shares outstanding represents 10 percent ownership. At the same time, 10 shares in a company with 1,000 shares represents only 1 percent ownership. Obviously, someone with 1 percent ownership won't be able to significantly influence his investment.

So the best stock investment you can make is in a company in which you are in a position to influence the success of that company. This is just another form of investing in yourself. The people who make the most money on stock investment are those who invest in themselves.

Investing money can be an intimidating subject to those who don't have experience in doing it. Yet, the investment principle is fairly simple. You have to invest money, not spend it, to become wealthy. This means avoiding a lifestyle that will consume the money that ought to be invested. Then, good investments don't happen overnight; you have to be a long ranger. And finally, often the best investment is in yourself—investing in your own sweat equity, your own business, and your own dreams.

NINE
THE PEOPLE PRINCIPLE

An organization called SRI International recently did a three-year, $2 million research study called VALS, the study of values and lifestyles in America. They determined there were four basic groups of people in this country.

1. The "need-driven" group. These are people who live hand-to-mouth and usually don't have much in the way of savings or financial security. They are driven by their needs.

There are two kinds of need-driven people: the "survivor" and the "sustainer." The survivor is at the bottom rung of the American social ladder. He is almost below welfare. He wonders how he will survive every single day. A lot of elderly and ethnic minorities fall into this subcategory. They live with great pressure every day just to survive.

Just above the survivor is the "sustainer," the worker who collects his pay once a week or every two weeks. He has a little bit more—maybe he rents a small apartment, has a TV, owns an old car, and basically just hangs on. The "sustainer" carries around a great deal of anger, and is often involved in street drugs and street crime. Sometimes the sustainer is street smart and proud of it. The children of the "sustainer" become hardened early in life because of the economic realities with which they have to live.

2. *The "outer-directed" group.* These people are more goal-centered. They are made up of three subgroups: belongers, emulators, and achievers.

"Belongers" are really the largest single group dealt with in this study. They tend to be aging, conservative, content, intensely patriotic middle Americans. They comprise 35 percent of the U.S. adult population. (Survivors, for example, make up only 4 percent and sustainers about 11 percent.) The average age of "belongers" is in the middle fifties. A lot of them have blue-collar jobs, healthy savings accounts, and they really do form much of the backbone of this country. They are not great achievers, but they are stable and solid and tend as a group to be happy.

Just above the belongers is a group called the "emulators." Emulators are usually young, ambitious, and flashy. They're trying to break into the achiever system. A lot of these emulators are children of belongers. The only problem with emulators is they want to be achievers, but they don't quite know how. They want to do it but they don't know what pattern to follow. They get most of their ideas of achievement and success from television, motion pictures, and romance magazines. They think that to be an achiever you've got to live like the people on "Dallas" or "Dynasty." Consequently, the emulators rarely become achievers because they try to emulate or copy an achiever lifestyle without doing achiever work. They're ambitious and hard working, but they blow their money on lifestyle. They want to spend their money where it shows. They want to dazzle you. They tend to be short-termers. Very few "emulators" become achievers. Most of them will spend a lot of money, will look good, maybe have good sales accounts, and then slip back into the "belonger" class, maybe even lower than that as they get toward retirement age.

"Achievers" make up some 22 percent of the U.S. adult population. Achievers tend to be more middle-aged, more prosperous, more self-assured. They are whom you think of as the leaders and builders of the American dream. They are people who have worked hard, built companies, are self-employed. Achievers believe in hard work; they believe you don't get rich quick. They know that to attain an achiever lifestyle, you have to pay an achiever price.

3. *The "inner-directed" group.* The "inner-directed" are people who have their own reasons for doing things, reasons you may not always be able to figure out. There are three types of people in the inner-directed groups.

The "I am me" group is usually young, right out of college, and impulsive. They will do a lot of crazy stuff, such as going to disco clubs every night.

They're strung out on pleasure. A lot of times they are from good families that have made some money, and they have some education, but they want to live it up right now.

The "experientials" are from wealthy achiever families. They are big on education, but they don't really care much unless they are dealing with the simple things of life. They want to live close to nature, they espouse natural childbirth, eat natural foods, like living out in the woods or close to the beach. There's nothing wrong with that. The problem is that experientials don't care much about anything else.

Finally, "society-conscious" people are usually inner-directed by causes, usually liberal causes. Society-conscious people spend lots of time and money supporting and leading movements dealing with contemporary issues and problems.

4. *The "integrated" group.* Integrateds are a combination of experientials, the society-conscious, and achievers. They love the simple things of the natural outdoors like the experientials. Yet they are also society conscious and want to help people. As two percent of the adult population, they also are real achievers who make money and are very productive.

MIDDLE-CLASS ANXIETY

Each of these social categories is interesting and bears closer examination, but I want to focus on the emulator. Chances are, you are from a middle-class background and are some form of emulator. You know enough about success to want to copy it, but you have not yet grasped the secrets of building, hard work, and long-terming that achievers have discovered.

The danger for emulators, especially, in thinking about status and class, is that it will become too important. If you become overly worried about what level you've attained, you will keep yourself from growing because you will have become self-centered. Emulators really want the achiever life-style, but they tend to spend more time trying to look like an achiever than trying to be an achiever.

This is the gist of my point in this chapter: Middle-class people have the greatest level of status anxiety of any class group in America. Middle-class people are continually worried about whether they appear "upper class" enough. The interesting thing is that upper-class people—true achievers—don't worry about those things much at all.

A study profiled the typical middle-class woman. When she has guests over for dinner, they talk and chat. But the moment the guests sit down to dinner, they cease being the friends of this woman, and they become her audience. She feels that she must impress them. It's usually a matter of overkill—too many things on the table, overly formal arrangements, stuffy observation of formal etiquette, etc. She tries to impress them that she is in a superior social class, that she knows how a formal dinner should be conducted. What it creates is a stiff and awkward occasion, and people breathe a little easier when it's over.

Now, you probably come from a middle-class background, and I do too. So I don't mean this profile as a put-down. It's just a recognition that many people in the middle class, many people who are emulators according to the SRI study, are horrified at the thought of appearing lower class. They continually worry about it. They are overly concerned with appearances, with what people think of them, and with trying to demonstrate that they're socially superior.

Let me tell you that this becomes a hindrance to truly achieving success. Why? Because the future focus is wrong. The focus isn't on achieving something, but on appearing *as if one has achieved something.*

Here's a hypothetical example. Let's say you're sitting on an airplane. A flight attendant, a middle-class emulator, stands up and says something like this: "I would like to make a very special announcement at this time, if I may have your attention. We are glad to have you on board, but we want you to know that the lighting of smoking materials is henceforth prohibited in the front lavatories." The flight attendant sounds very proper and stylish and upper-class. But do you know how an upper-class person in all likelihood would communicate the same message? "No smoking in the bathrooms." A true achiever wouldn't waste time and certainly wouldn't worry about impressing anybody. The achiever has a goal and goes after it. The emulator's goal is to sound upper class.

You see this often in the matter of fashion and dress. You're on the same airplane. Across the aisle you see a boy and girl in their twenties. Both are wearing dirty, torn bluejeans. The boy's cotton shirt is faded and torn. They are wearing moccasins with no socks. Are they lower class, middle class, or upper class? The amazing thing is they most likely are lower class or upper class, but probably not middle class. Middle-class people tend to dress up for travel, especially when traveling by plane: image reigns. The upper class person usually dresses down, as comfortably as possible: practicality reigns.

Vocabulary is a dead giveaway. A clean-cut young man on that same plane is conversing with the man next to him. You hear words like "interface," "funding," "dialogue," "lifestyle," "bottom line." He's very serious. And this man is probably very middle class. He's using contemporary buzz words, vogue words, that will make him sound important.

I was in a restaurant recently and three tables away from us was a man talking in a loud voice about the stock market and his recommendations on what to do. He was making sure everybody around could hear him. He wanted everybody to know he was upper class, but everything he did indicated that he was an insecure, middle-class businessman.

Dr. Thomas Stanley, president of the Affluent Marketing Institute in Atlanta, said that "the true financial goal of most Americans is not to be rich, not to be affluent, and not to be wealthy. The true goal is to appear affluent and seem wealthy." In a way, calling someone an emulator is a nice way of calling someone a con artist. You're trying to be something you're not. You waste time and money "dressing up" like a rich man. But if you're truly thinking like the average millionaire in America today, you won't think about the trappings of success. You'll focus on the means toward achieving greater success—you'll pour your financial success back into your business, your goals. The real comfort to the achiever is not to have the Rolls Royce in the garage, but to know he can afford it if he wanted it. The real anxiety of the emulator is to have a Rolls Royce in the garage, to realize how much he wants and even needs it for his self-image, but to know that in fact he can't really afford it at all.

UPPER-CLASS SENSIBILITY

Whereas the middle class emulator tries so hard to impress, the upper-class achiever puts you at ease and builds you up. You see, the upper-class achiever has learned the people principle: that people are important to life, personal happiness, and success. You don't want to build yourself up at the expense of others; you don't want to make other people feel uncomfortable around you. Instead the true achiever wants to build friendships and strong personal connections.

Of course, there are exceptions to this. All of us

have encountered upper-class people who are obnoxious. However, in many cases they are usually children of achievers who have never really achieved themselves; they've inherited a lot of their money and don't understand the values and principles to work for it. But I believe you'll find that most *true* achievers will treat you with respect. They'll talk with you, listen to you, and be courteous.

I know these are generalizations, broad social stereotypes. But there is much truth in these stereotypes. The rare exception proves the rule. For you to be a true achiever, you have to forget about appearances. You need to shed your middle-class anxieties. You need to think, as many achievers do, about people and how important they are to you.

FRIENDSHIP BUILDERS

The Bible has a great deal to say about this. The character qualities of love, joy, gladness, peace, an even temper, kindness, goodness, gentleness, politeness, and self-control, among others, are qualities that Jesus Christ can help grow in your life when you encounter him personally. These qualities will help you deal directly and compassionately with other people. But if you're tied up in knots, always trying to prove your status, you'll never relax enough to find out what another person needs. You'll never achieve true success.

The little book *Seasons of Success*, contains nine friendship-builders that I find helpful and that I've tried to incorporate into my own life:

1. Go out of your way to help other people. Do things for them.

2. Always be dependable. Do what you say you'll do. Don't schedule for a party and cancel. That makes people feel as if you treated them with disrespect. It's better not to make the commitment than to make several commitments and fail to keep them.

3. Be tolerant and gracious. Be forgiving.

4. Don't dominate people. Be a friend, not a boss.

5. Be humble, be teachable.

6. Don't carry an attitude of superiority, an air of status. If you feel friendly toward people, you will project friendliness. If you project warmth or love, you'll project them. But if you feel superior, you will project that and they will pull away from you.

7. Always be completely honest in all of your business and personal dealings.

8. Don't use sarcasm, even when you are joking.

9. Don't make fun of other people.

Remember this, you're not trying to project an ice-cold image of the perfect person, the upper-class person, the person with great status. That's not your goal. You're trying to help others and build friendships. You want to sow lots of goodwill with people. You want to be a goodwill-sower and a friendship-builder. This is the key to the People Principle.

Part III
PRACTICAL STEPS
TO
FINANCIAL SUCCESS

TEN
BREAKING BUDGET BARRIERS

Most of you hunger for financial freedom. You are sick and tired of your financial battles because they're like a merry-go-round. You think you're going in circles. You're not getting anywhere. You have the same crises every year. The same difficulty every few months. The same problem every April 15th. You don't know how to break free from the negative patterns that you have found yourself trapped in.

If it's any comfort, let me tell you that I've been there before. I've made a lot of mistakes—financial mistakes—in my life. I didn't realize in the early days that when I moved out of the alley and into the oldest house up in the neighborhood, that no matter how much I would do to fix it up, it wouldn't appreciate. I would have been better off buying a smaller home in a better neighborhood. It was a mistake, but I learned from it. I've made a lot of mistakes in my time. But now I figure that those mistakes should count for something! So, as I explain to you some of the basic barriers that you face and how to break them down, realize that a lot of what I'm telling you I learned the hard way. I've been through it myself.

In any case, I'm going to help you get off the merry-go-round. In the next chapter I'm going to show you how to do a personal financial analysis and set up a budget. I know this is something you'd probably rather not do. In fact, most people are budget-avoiders.

I have identified ten reasons why most people do not make budgets. A budget is an essential tool to effective money management. But a lot of people don't keep them because they don't like them, and they don't like them because there are these eleven obstacles, or barriers, to making a budget.

Budget barrier #1—lack of training. It may be that you just don't know how to manage money and successfully organize your finances. You didn't get the training in college, school, or church, and you didn't get it from your parents. (You may have learned as little from your parents about money as you learned about sex.) Chances are, your parents haven't sat down with you and warned you about the dangers of credit cards, or the nature of interest rates, or how you should invest your savings. The fact is, most of you are in the same boat, but you don't know it. No one teaches these things, and yet they're among the most important, most fundamental building blocks of success.

Budget barrier #2—self-centeredness. I heard of a woman attending one of our business meetings who said to one of our leaders, "Hey, I need a budget. Tell me how to do it. Tell me how I can save more money." The woman had a whole list of questions, and the leader began to tell her she could do this and that, how to write things down, and so on. Midway through the conversation, the seminar leader became very suspicious of her motives. Finally she said, "I have come to this business meeting and I'm very excited about the training here, but I really can't afford to come to any others because I just don't have enough extra cash to keep coming. I want to come to the business meetings, but I can't afford it."

The leader told her she could make a financial plan so she could afford to come to the meetings, and he asked her what kind of plan she thought would be appropriate. When he asked her that question, he thought she would say, "Oh, you mean a budget." But she didn't say that. Instead she replied, "I'll borrow the money." The seminar leader told her that's not what he meant. He told her to budget for her business functions and business expenses, and to eliminate all kinds of costly activities. And she became negative instantly, pulling back from the seminar leader. She said, "Oh, no. I don't want to do that."

She was selfish. She didn't want to budget and build for her future because she didn't want to give up something she wanted.

So you're faced with a similar decision right now.

How much do you want financial freedom? How much do you want to be able to sleep at night knowing that your bills are paid and your debts are manageable and you're free? How much do you want that kind of liberation? Or do you choose instead to be selfish like that woman? And do you refrain from budgeting because there are some things you don't want to give up? Listen. You've got to grow up and make a mature decision. Do you want freedom or don't you?

Budget barrier #3—laziness. Many budgets don't work because people get lazy and don't maintain them on a regular basis. There are no easy solutions to this budget barrier. It's simply a matter of deciding to discipline yourself to do it.

It's easier to discipline yourself in this area if you visualize what can be your budget future. Think of the future times when you'll pay bills with confidence, when your budget categories are working, and when you're really saving and investing money. Visualize the freedom you'll feel and the positive results of maintaining a budget, and you'll find that your laziness will evaporate.

Budget barrier #4—entitlement. What this means is you don't think it's fair that you have to have a budget. You wonder why you have to go through the discipline and inconvenience of budgeting out your life. You have this great sense of entitlement, a feeling that you deserve to be free from financial pressures without having to do anything about it. Sociologists are calling this the entitlement generation because everybody feels entitled to everything. You feel you deserve the biggest house and the most powerful luxury car. You feel you deserve everything, but the truth is—and this is a biblical principle—that you don't deserve anything. As I read the book of Proverbs, I find that it is jam-packed with many incredible business principles right from the heart of God. All these verses just pour out all kinds of practical guidance. Over and over Proverbs says not to forget to work, don't forget to earn your way. So you're not "entitled." Some of you have a major budget barrier because you resent having to do the budget. It's just not fair, you say, but fairness has nothing to do with it. I remember listening to my children playing with other children. Every time they got into a fix they didn't like, the first words they screamed were "It's not fair." Well, adults are the same way. You see, fairness actually has nothing to do with it, and if you carry that into your adult attitude, it will stop you from financial maturity. You cannot afford that and you don't want that.

Budget barrier #5—injured pride and embarrassment. You feel that by having to make a budget, you are admitting failure. You're embarrassed by that. You have a sense of wounded pride. It may be that you actually have failed financially in certain areas. You need to realize that many people have failed financially. I have. But I've learned from those experiences, and I've moved forward.

So, again you need to make a decision. Do you want injured pride or do you want to make more money? Will you avoid budgeting because you don't want to admit failure in an area, or do you want to be free and pay your debts, standing straight and tall with self-respect and personal dignity? The more you feel you have failed in a particular area, the more you try to prove yourself. Now, you know you do that. You try to compensate and try to make up for it, and say, "Hey, nothing is wrong." That's why so often in marriage counseling, the man resists coming to counseling because he doesn't want to admit there is a problem in his marriage. The most intelligent thing you can do is to work on some weak area in you life, tackle it, face your fear, and do something about it.

Budget barrier #6—doubt. Will your budget work? You may not be sure it will work, or if it will change anything, because in the past you've had so many hopes dashed. You've had so many promises broken, and your finances are still in wretched condition, and you want somebody to please help you.

Hey, I've got great news for you. You can win on this. A budget is the first step to achieving financial freedom. If you are diligent in maintaining your budget, if you overcome these budget barriers, it will work for you.

Budget barrier #7—arrogance. This is the attitude of "I don't need any help." It is similar to wounded pride, but it's more aggressive. Arrogance is hot and angry. Arrogance is "Get out of my face, I can handle it myself." Hey, how have you handled it so far?

Budget barrier #8—defeatism. Sometimes you get the feeling that you just can't win, that the problem is too big. Some of you have big debts and you've dug a hole, and it's taken you a long, long time to get in the fix you're in, and it may take you a while to get out of it. But you can't let defeatism stop you from making your budget. You may feel that it's overwhelming, but let me tell you that some people have been in far worse financial condition and have wound up winning and achieving. You can do it!

Budget barrier #9—gloom and doom. This is the attitude of "Well, OK, I'll grit my teeth and do the budget. I'll do it, but I don't like it." And you think there will be no more fun in life. You see a budget as bondage, and you think it will be horrible. Now, it will require some changes in personal discipline, but it's not the gloom that you fear. And it will present you with some personal challenges, but it's not the doom you expect. Be honest. You probably don't make a budget because you think it will eliminate the fun parts of life. It's not necessarily so. You have to look past your initial impression of a budget and visualize the results that you will get from executing a budget faithfully.

Budget barrier #10—inertia. Inertia is resistance to change. Inertia, in physics, is the law that says if something is moving, it's harder to stop it from moving, or if something is sitting still, it takes more energy to push it and get it going. It's another way of saying resistance to change. Many of you do not like your current financial condition, but it's familiar to you. Because you're familiar with the mess you're in, there is some natural resistance—

inertia—against making a change. You may be in a bad mess, but at least it's your mess, and you know the mess real well. In fact, in counseling we're taught that one reason why some people don't leave very bad family situations after they've grown up is because they're so comfortable with them. They may be full of maladjustment and the health of the family may be in horrible shape, but they're just used to it. It's the same with your budget. Sometimes you don't make a budget because of resistance to change, and you're inclined to keep things as they are.

There was a woman doing a seminar on how to change your life. Early in the seminar, the lady said, "You know, I think it's stupid to watch the evening news at night. It's a waste of time. It's negative, and I think it's stupid. I don't believe anybody ought to do it." Her audience up to this point had been very polite and receptive and had liked her material. But suddenly the audience members reacted with hostility. A man stood up and said, "I like to watch the news and it's nobody's business if I like it." Another woman stood and said, "Well, I like it too, and I don't think you have any right to tell us that it's stupid to watch it." And the seminar leader watched and listened for fifteen minutes as one after another stood to oppose her statement about watching the evening news. Then she asked them a question: Did they feel negative after the news? Most audience members admitted they did. Yet they remained adamant about the value of watching the news. After a short while, the seminar leader laughed. "Do you realize what you have just done?" she asked. "You have illustrated what I've been telling you the whole seminar—that the reason most of you do not change is because you've got a resistance to change itself. You don't want to change anything, even if it's good for you." They all laughed at that point, and, well, you get the message. Some of you resist change. You know you need a budget, and you know you need to change and do something about the mess you're in. But still you resist change. It's human nature. It's human inertia.

Well, I've identified the common budget barriers, and I hope that by doing so I've given you some encouragement. But I'm not going to leave you there. You need motivation and practical advice to get you going. That's what we'll tackle next.

ELEVEN
DOING A PERSONAL FINANCIAL ANALYSIS

Now I'm going to help you do a personal financial analysis. It's not so hard to *do*, sometimes just hard to *face*. But you're making reality decisions now, right?!

Get yourself a pencil and a tablet of paper. Write on one sheet "Income." On a second sheet, write "Expenses." On a third sheet, write "Debts." And on a fourth sheet, write "Assets." (You might want to allow several sheets of paper for each list.) Let's look at each list in more detail:

1. Income. List all your sources of income. Figure your take-home pay (not your gross pay!). Add in any other sources of income—regular payments for outside work that you do. Include payments from trust funds, interest from savings accounts, money market funds, etc. Be conservative; don't overestimate; don't include income that you're not sure about (bonuses, gifts, etc.). If you are surprised along the way, you want to be pleasantly surprised!

2. Expenses. Do this in two stages. First, list all the categories of expenses that you have each month. Looking through the statement portion of your checkbook will quickly give you most of your expense categories. This should include rent/mortgage, utilities, food, clothing, and other obvious things. It also should include easily forgotten categories such as the annual physical with the doctor, dental checkups, eyeglass prescriptions, etc. You may have to guess at some expense categories, anticipate what might happen during the next twelve months.

Your second stage of the expense list is to actually put down the amount of expenditure in each category. You won't know precisely what certain things cost each month (utilities, for example), but you should have a close estimate. Estimate a little high if you're in doubt.

3. Debts. Debts could be listed as expenses, but it can be valuable to list them separately. These are payments you make each month that you want to eliminate in the future. Debts should include credit cards, car payments, installment loans, etc. Debt reduction will become one of your first goals in your financial plan.

Again, go through a two-stage process: First, list your debt categories; second, fill in the numbers. You may list the monthly minimum payments for your credit cards, but also put down the total balance. You'll need to pay off more than the minimum each month in order to get ahead.

4. Assets. Finally, list your assets—the things

you own and how much they're worth. Include the equity you have in your house, the current "blue book" value of your car, jewelry, furniture, etc.

Now, we want to figure your net worth. Add up your assets, add up your expenses and debts together, subtract one from the other—and that's your net worth. You may actually have a negative net worth—a lot of people (too many) do—which means simply that you owe more than you own. Your ultimate goal in making your financial plan will be to increase your net worth. You want that negative sign to change into a positive sign.

Next we need to figure your monthly balance. Add up your expenses and your debts together, then subtract that figure from your monthly income. You may wind up with a negative balance, which means you spend more than you make each month. Usually the negative amount winds up getting added to a credit card or installment debt account, which makes the balance the next month even more negative.

Finally, we have to develop our budget. This time take a new piece of paper. List all your expenses and debts and their monthly equivalents. Figure out what expenses might be cut back. Remember you have to reduce your expenses so as not to exceed income. You may actually have fun eliminating some expenses: maybe you don't really need four magazine subscriptions; perhaps you can do without the YMCA membership; consider reducing your car repair costs by doing some maintenance work yourself. If you go through this process, you'll find that you'll feel better as you're doing it. You're taking control!

Of course, some decisions will be harder. You may have to change your eating habits—eat less, eat less expensively. Maybe you need to get by with one car instead of two. Ouch! But the point is, if your monthly balance is negative, you can't afford the lifestyle you're leading.

Making a budget may take a while. You and your spouse will need to negotiate specific expenses. You'll need to work back and forth between expenses and income to see where you are in the process. It'll require a lot of adjustment, fiddling, tinkering. But in the end you'll have a budget—a financial plan that will allow you to control your life and future!

TIPS FOR MAKING THE PROCESS EASIER

Someone once said that when you turn a big ship around, you don't turn it around quickly. It takes a long time to see the effects of the turning. In making your budget, you have started steering the ship in the opposite direction. But like a large vessel at sea, it may take some time before you see the full effect of it. But if you don't act now, the ship will take even longer to turn around. You must begin now.

Let me suggest some ways that will help make the budgeting process easier:

1. *Commit the budget situation to God.* I really believe that by turning to God through faith in

Jesus Christ, you can release a greater power that can accomplish great things in your life. In fact, I have experienced it myself. It's awesome. It's amazing. A supernatural power that is not psychological or not emotional, but a power from God. I believe this power can work in your financial planning. In fact, I think it's essential that you bring spiritual power to the essential decisions you are making in the budgeting process. I think you'll find that this is a major element in the success of your budgeting plan.

2. Record every penny you spend for one month. That may sound like lightweight work, but if you've ever done it, you know it's tough stuff. You need to do this before budgeting, before doing a financial analysis. Ron tells of the time he and his wife, Amy, went through this process. They recorded every dime they spent, every penny, for thirty days. I mean everything. If they bought a newspaper for twenty-five cents, they recorded it. If they bought chewing gum, they recorded it. If they spent money on a toll or a phone call or eating out, they recorded it all—even the tip.

Ron says now that they couldn't have accomplished a successful financial plan without this month of discipline and financial record-keeping. To make good budgeting decisions, you have to know exactly what you're spending, where your money is going. Ron says:

> *Amy and I were shocked to realize the waste*
> *that we were experiencing. We wasted money*

that we didn't even know we wasted. I thought I knew what I spent but when I actually looked at it, we were spending more on things than I thought we were. You've got to know where you're spending. There is no substitute for this discipline. You have to have accurate analysis, sound record-keeping. So for one month, Amy and I recorded little notebooks and recorded every cent, every dime. At the end of that month, we knew what we had to do.

3. *Eliminate ruthlessly.* In paring your budget to the bone, you must spare nothing. Remember your purpose is debt elimination, freedom, control. You may find it's a two-step process: first, you cut out things you know you can live without; second, you cut out things you don't think you can live without. It's hard! But don't get discouraged.

There is the true story of a pastor who, when he retired from the ministry, had $1 million cash. However, he had never made more than $8,000 a year in his life. How did he do it? He eliminated ruthlessly. In this case, his goal was to retire with financial freedom. He also wanted a certain amount to give to causes he believed in. He figured a million dollars would do it. That became his goal. This is not a made up story—it's been checked out. He really did it—he saved $1 million in his lifetime, mostly because he minimized his own expenses and saved and invested almost everything he earned.

4. *Be prepared for your first quick failure.* There

will be failures—even right off the bat—because you have not done this before. You are just a budget beginner, just starting your freedom plan, so you will have immediate failures. Be prepared psychologically to handle them.

Again, Ron tells of the experience he and Amy had:

> *When we started our first budget, we knew (or thought we knew) what we were going to spend for a month. Then Amy and I decided after four days to check it out and see how we were doing. When I added up what we had spent, we had spent in four days 75 percent of our month's budget. Isn't that incredible? We budgeted out what we could live on for a month, what we had to do to pay off debts, and we had spent 75 percent of that in four days. So we started our budget with a big failure— but we didn't stop, and that's the key. We didn't quit and ultimately we won!*

5. *Establish early that this is a true partnership— that you as a husband and wife are in this together.* You got into debt together, and you're going to get out of debt together. Too often the husband prepares the budget, cutting corners on a lot of expense categories in ways that the wife finds difficult to swallow. These situations doom the success of the budget process. The wife then feels straitjacketed and trapped. It never works. You have to have a partnership. You don't want to

blame each other or make the other totally responsible for how it's going to work. You have to pull together.

6. *Learn the difference between supportive friends and friendly saboteurs.* You won't be able to confide in everyone about your budget plan. Some of your friends will want to undermine you. They may be in the same boat as you are but unwilling to change. They may try to coerce you into spending in areas that you haven't budgeted. They may even in very small ways belittle and ridicule what you are doing. They become friendly saboteurs. So you need to be careful who you tell your plans to. This can even include family members. Not all family members are going to be supportive, so learn the difference.

7. *Focus on your financial goals.* Your goals will get you through the dark times, through the withdrawal when you miss all the money you were spending before your budget. That's the only way you can have the personal energy to make this thing work. Keep on focusing and concentrating on the freedom you're going to experience.

8. *Record all debt reductions and payoffs.* Celebrate the gradual achievement of your debt-reduction goals. Put charts up—in the kitchen, the study, all over—and record the payments you make. Re-calculate the balance you owe to show it coming down.

9. *Streamline your living.* Even after you've gone through the difficult process of budgeting, explore ways to cut your expenses further. Make a game

of it. Try to come up with a savings tip each day. Skip a meal a week. Cut down on the hot water you use. Try to outdo yourselves in your savings strategies.

Ron tells of when he and Amy were in Florida just after they started their budget, and they went to Disney World. This was already in the budget and paid for, but they knew resort food was expensive. So Amy brought sandwiches, ice water, tea, and celery, and they sat in the parking lot of Epcot Center, eating their lunch before they went in. It would have been fun to eat there at Disney, but it did not fit their budget. They learned to streamline their living.

10. Learn to handle breakdowns properly. Don't let breakdowns discourage you. No budget works 100 percent of the time. Just climb back on and continue working at it. Don't quit and give up. Instead get onto your budget again. It's like dieting—and most of us have some experience with that. If you fail on your diet after two weeks and eight pounds, what do you do? Your goal is to lose thirty pounds and you've already lost eight. Do you say, "I am an abject, horrible failure. I might as well eat what I want"? Do you then go on an enormous eating binge and gain fifteen more pounds? How foolish. No, you get back on your diet. After all, you still lost eight pounds. If you get right back on, you will reach the remaining twenty-two-pound loss and reach your goal.

The same thing is true with a budget. If you have a breakdown after two or three weeks, don't say,

"I knew it. I knew we couldn't do it." And by all means don't blame your wife or husband. Don't be angry, but get back on your budget because already you are closer to your financial goals than you would be if you hadn't had the budget the two previous weeks.

11. Don't legalize your budget. Don't make it into just a bunch of rules. That can make budgeting tedious and joyless. Remember this is a freedom plan. If you budget yourself to spend $18.32 on groceries on a given day, and you add it all up at the register and spend $19.00, you don't go home in despair and discouragement. You went over by 68 cents. So what? You're still closer to your goal than you would have been if you had gone into the grocery store with no budget and spent $30.00 on potato chips and Cokes. Listen, don't legalize your budget. Be a little flexible. This is not a prison. Remember, it's not just a budget but a freedom plan.

12. Don't expect the budget to solve all your problems overnight. Don't think, "Well now I have a budget so I can relax financially." Hold on—that's not true. Some people think that since they have made the budget, the battle is over. No, the budget is a map, a plan, a way to reach your ultimate objective, and a way to get where you want to go. You still have to drive there yourself.

13. Develop a knack for inexpensive fun. You might say that the key word is "inexpensive" because we're talking money management here, but I don't think so. I think the key word is "fun."

There is a book titled *His Needs, Her Needs*, which I recommend highly. In this book, the author, Dr. Harley, suggests that a husband and wife, to help them discover activities they might do together, make lists. He suggests the wife make a list of twenty-five things she'd like to do. (And in this case twenty-five inexpensive things that she would like to try.) And the husband makes a list of twenty-five inexpensive fun things he would like to do as well. Then the couple gets together and looks at the list of fifty items. Many will be different, of course, but it's surprising how many are the same, appearing on both lists. This has a double benefit, it not only saves you money, but it brings you closer as a husband and wife. You'll come to love life together even more. So, develop lists of inexpensive fun interests.

14. Develop safety valves. That is, sometimes go ahead and spend money that's not in the budget. Shocked? Well, sometimes you need to have that release. Be careful with this; you could make it an excuse, and you can't afford for that to happen. But once in a while, splurge. Enjoy yourselves, and then get back on the budget. One analyst uses the term "mad money."

Maybe you ought to build into the budget some money that you can spend without accounting for it to the other person. Maybe it's like paying yourselves a personal allowance. Provide in the budget some money your spouse can spend without having to be accountable to you for it, and vice versa.

15. Learn a new attitude toward rewards. In other words, make the reward of your budget pay off the debts. Do you see the power of that? If you stay on the budget two months, don't reward yourself with a spending binge, but reward yourself with paying off bills. After you pay off bills, reward yourself with saving money. Remember saving money is a freedom fund to buy what you want and make your dreams come true. The payoff becomes the payoff—the emotional payoff (a reward) becomes the actual financial payoff of eliminating the debt. That means you don't get into deeper debt as a reward. You want to re-channel every reward back into your goal of making the budget work.

16. Be accountable to someone. Accountability must be voluntary, but it's also necessary. Find someone who understands and supports what you're trying to do. Find a way of making contact with this person on a regular basis and sharing your budget experience with this person. It doesn't have to be a formal relationship. In fact, an informal friendship can work even better. But if you know you're accountable to someone else for your budget success, you will have a greater incentive for it to succeed.

Finally, I want you to remember two things. A budget itself is very simple. Don't be intimidated by it. It's just a plan. The key to all of this is committed action. You *have* to do it. You have got to have a freedom plan. Make it work. Your dreams and your goals not only can come true, they will come true.

TWELVE
COMMON SENSE ABOUT MANAGING MONEY

1. Never pay retail for anything you can buy wholesale. If you have to go to a retail place to buy something, such as an automobile, figure out what the seller's profit is and try to cut it down to a minimum. Try to come as close to the cost as you can, especially on big purchases.

2. Never finance anything too long. Avoid paying too much interest. You should finance only a house or car.

3. A car should be financed for no more than two to three years if possible. Don't buy all the luxury options if you have to finance it. You don't need the moon roof or wire wheels. You're buying transportation. Make sure that it's transportation and not living quarters—at least until you can pay cash for it.

4. A home should never be financed for more than ten to fifteen years. The payments aren't going to change as much as most people think. They think if you finance it for thirty years that you cut the

payment by a third or a half, but it's only a matter of a few hundred dollars' difference. Get a financial chart and check it out. If I'm thirty years old, and I take a fifteen-year mortgage on a house and decide to live in that house the rest of my life, by the time I'm forty-five I've got the house paid for. But most people finance for thirty or thirty-five years, and they pay it off when they're sixty or sixty-five. Then if they have a financial reversal in their life or a health problem, they could lose the home they spent most of their life paying for.

5. Work your way up to things. Don't stretch yourself too far. You don't need to have your dream house and your dream lifestyle now. In fact, you can't afford to live that way.

6. Don't use credit cards except as a receipt. If you're going to finance something, pay it off in thirty days and avoid the interest. Credit cards range from 15 to 25 percent interest. If you're paying credit minimums month after month like the average person, you wind up paying for purchases long after those items have worn out.

7. Go without little things. Save and save and save to buy the big things. Buy brick and mortar. Buy something that contains its value. Things that depreciate will cost you dearly in the long run.

8. Never spend more than $5.00 to $10.00 for an average meal out. You can find reasonable places to get good food, but don't pay for somebody's wallpaper, carpet, doormen, and all the yuppy extras that people pay for. All food normally comes from the same wholesalers. If

somebody is putting too many sauces on it to sell it fancy, it may be because you're not getting it as fresh as you would from an establishment that does volume and offers meals at lower prices.

9. Don't buy designer clothes. You can normally find the same clothes for half the price without a designer label on it. Don't buy the name brand that a store has. For instance, Bill Jones Clothing Store sells Bill Jones suits. The suit is a generic make that the store buys from a wholesaler; then they slap their own label on it and hike the price. You're paying for the Bill Jones advertisement. Go to a wholesale place and buy the same suit at 50 percent off. When you buy designer clothes, you're paying for their advertising.

10. Look for furniture outlets where you can buy a whole living room for the same price as a chair. There are places to buy where you can get 50 percent off some merchandise that is also sold at normal retail establishments.

11. Pump your own gas. Over the course of a year, it'll save you hundreds of dollars, and you could probably use the exercise anyway. Find a cheap place to buy gas and get into the habit of fueling up at the same place all the time.

12. The more expensive something is, the more you ought to shop around for the best deal.

13. Never buy things on emotion. Go home and think about it for a couple days before you go back and make your decision. If you buy purchases today on emotion and you go home and think about it, you probably wouldn't have bought it after you thought

about it. Not buying is like saving money.

14. A third off is not a savings if you didn't need it in the first place.

15. Brand names don't always communicate the same things to all people. You may be thinking that you're buying quality in buying a particular brand name, when in fact some people don't think of that brand in such a good light.

16. Use furniture until it wears out. Sure, buy a new piece if you need it, but keep the old furniture and use it in a different room until it's worn out, or consider recovering it.

17. If you don't shop around, you're foolish. Most salesmen will tell you about the guy that didn't ask for a discount and who wrote a check for retail. A fool and his money are soon parted. It's people that are trying to pretend they have money that don't ask for discounts. People who have money normally look for the best deal. Even large corporations shop around, taking bids on things they are going to purchase. When I worked for a large corporation and had a company car, I had to get three bids on cars to be my company car. So you better believe I'm doing that when I go look to buy a car for myself or my family.

18. Most people are trying to "look status." They play wealthy instead of being wealthy. I would rather play a low profile and have a high net worth than play a high profile and have a low net worth. The sooner I build net worth, the fewer years I have to put in. If I just spend everything I have and don't manage it well, then I have to keep making more

and more money to live as well as I've been living.

19. Everything you build should be long term. Consider the woman who buys a new hat every time she's depressed. She buys a high that lasts for only a few hours, and it's an expensive high. Some people buy clothes that way, or even cars that way, and they buy on credit because they don't have the money on hand. They develop financial depression, and then they add to their previous depression, which compounds the original problem.

20. The majority of adult Americans are poor money managers. That's why so many make better money than their parents did, yet wind up struggling so much. The average young American couple today tries to obtain by the age of twenty-five what their parents had when they were fifty.

21. Don't buy depreciating items on credit. When you walk out of a clothing store, those clothes you just bought lose probably 90 percent of their value. A used suit has very little value next to a new suit. Furniture is the same. Used furniture has very low value next to new furniture. A used bed isn't worth much to anyone else but you.

22. People fail in life because they fail to plan. You've got to plan to succeed. A man doesn't wake up and all of a sudden a bell rings and he's a millionaire. He planned for it. He started being worth $5,000, then $10,000, then $50,000, then $100,000—it becomes a multiplying process. It's like if you took a penny a day and doubled it, at the end of 30 days you'd have an astronomical amount.

23. Too many people don't understand delayed

gratification. Why not save money and get something when you can afford it, instead of borrowing money to buy when you think other people think you ought to have it? You can be the best-dressed guy in town for ten years, or you can buy good clothes that look as good to the average person at wholesale, but spend less money and save more. If you do that with all your purchases throughout your life, then ten years from now you'll find your net worth has grown tremendously. If you make $100,000 a year and put 50 percent of it aside, and after taxes you're in the 20 percent income tax bracket, you pay $20,000 for taxes. You have $80,000, live on $40,000 and invest $40,000. That invested $40,000 will multiply.

24. Too many people don't understand the importance of net worth. It's the measure of getting ahead. Let's say you make $120,000 a year. At the end of ten years (let's assume no inflation and no pay raises), you've made $1,200,000. But if you spent it all, you literally have nothing. You've worn out your cars, rented homes, gone through clothes and furniture. You have no net worth. However, let's suppose you took your money and lived on $40,000, paid $30,000 in taxes, and invested $50,000. If you invest that $50,000 for ten years, you're worth half a million dollars (more if you count interest). Now, if you put a down payment on real estate at $50,000 a year into a project at 20 percent down and financed it over ten years, then ten years from now that first $50,000 becomes worth a quarter of a million. If there is inflation, it could be worth $400,000. After ten years

of using your money this way, you could be worth a couple million dollars.

25. You make money work for you by first working for your money. It's sweat equity. It doesn't matter how you work—whether you're a doctor, a lawyer, a minister, or a mill worker—that's your own sweat. A successful person works sweat equity, then they can afford to hire other people to work sweat equity for them.

26. A lot of people put so much value on lifestyle early in their lives that they steal from their life-style in their later years. They financially rape their future by creating bills they will have to pay for the rest of their life.

27. Too many people put too much emphasis on education. Most people who get a lot of education end up working for people without an education whose real education is experience and common sense.

28. Keep your energy level high. A lot of people keep their gas tank on their car empty. But I try to keep my gas tank full because that in itself is saving money. If I run out of gas, I have a towing bill, I have to walk, I've lost time. If I keep my gas tank full and never let it go below half, then I never have to spend my time worrying about getting to a gas station, and I can keep my mind creative. In the same way, my dream tank, which keeps the energy flowing in my system, is something I try always to keep full. I always have enough dream to keep my motivation to discipline myself. It's energy pure and simple. Instead of working for energy to pay for luxuries I've bought in the past,

I'm using my energy to gain the money so I can pay cash for something I want. I keep my gas tank full. I also keep my dream tank full.

29. Don't let anybody steal your dreams. Your dreams are vital. They should be good dreams. They should be dreams that not only help you but help others.

30. People can't succeed without helping others succeed. When you succeed, you need assistants, employees, coworkers, maybe partners. You create jobs. You need services so you create income from others and help their business grow. If you're doing several millions of dollars a year in business, you're buying millions of dollars' worth of raw materials or finished merchandise from other companies, other people.

32. The stock market is something you have to babysit. I have tried investing in the stock market several times. You have to develop an expertise. You have to take the market's temperature every day. You've got to be very brilliant, or very lucky, or very blessed to make it in the stock market. Most people don't. I would rather invest in real estate because that market doesn't normally go up and down so fast. So, I would rather look where a town is growing and buy land or buildings in the growth pattern. That way I can relax, knowing it's going to appreciate.

33. Invest in yourself and in your own business. I like to invest in my own business because that's the area of my expertise. I know it's going to make money because it's well managed!

34. The greatest thing about land is they don't make any more of it.

35. A lot of people want to have the biggest home in the neighborhood. It's smarter to have one of the smaller homes in the neighborhood because if it's a nice neighborhood, the smaller home will appreciate faster than the biggest home.

36. I despise the guys who criticize to minimize the enterprise of other guys whose enterprise made them rise above the guys that criticize. A lot of people are going to be critical of you when you're successful. You've done what they wanted to do and thought about doing but didn't do. And, yes, anybody could have done it, but you're the one who had the guts to step out and really do it.

37. The average person does not truly know the value of a dollar.

38. Everybody starts out average. We talk about equality. Nobody is equal. Everybody has talents that are unique. There is no equality in life. One guy is six-five. Another is five-six. One is white, one is black, one is yellow, one is red. We all have different backgrounds, come from different homes. You are what you make yourself.

39. Most millionaires are common men with uncommon thinking. Common-sense thinking is the way people thought in the thirties and forties. Today it's called"conservatism."

40. The person I respect most is an honest person who has made his money morally.

THIRTEEN
THE SPIRITUAL SECRET OF TRUE SUCCESS

Cotton Mather, the early colonial Puritan leader, was the dominant spiritual influence of his generation. Mather is representative of the biblical beliefs that built America's extraordinary success. He wrote: "A Christian at work may glorify God by doing good for and getting good for himself. . . . I tell you with diligence, a man may do marvelous things. Young man, work hard where you are. Work hard while you're young. You will reap the effects of it when you are old. Yea, how can you ordinarily enjoy any rested night if you have not been well at work in the day? Let your business engross most of your time."

It is important for you to know that Mather never neglected his spiritual disciplines. Nor did he urge anyone else to do so. The daily worship of God was vital to his life. His belief in the inerrant inspiration of the Bible was complete. He never doubted the Almighty God's supreme authority in all of life. He also saw no contradiction in a combination of active spirituality and the energetic pursuit of personal and business success.

Why the brief history lesson? Because for some the idea of financial success without spiritual compromise is tough to swallow. You think it is always an either/or situation.

It is our firm contention that this perspective is not based on an accurate understanding of the Bible's teaching on success and money.

The Bible, of course, warns of the abuses of wealth and the dangers of human success. The Proverbs caution you to skirt the pitfall of arrogant pride; to avoid the trap of laziness; to steer away from self-centered relationships; to choose a positive, optimistic approach to life over a bleak, negative, fearful orientation. They tell you to be honest; that cheating will catch up with you; that kindness, love, and generosity are surer roads to long-term success than lying, gossip, and unfair criticism.

What about the man or woman on Wall Street who is at the top of glamor and power but is later indicted for illegal activities? Is this genuine success? Obviously, money and prestige can be temporary if one does not have the character to maintain success.

Can you be happy with the knowledge that your "success" has come at the cost of shattered people, disillusioned children, bitter marriage partners, and serious personal compromise?

This is why the Bible is the true source of

wisdom. You want success you can believe in, success you can be proud of. You want a success that will not destroy to people you love, a success philosophy you can pass to your children and grandchildren without fear.

The Bible is the foundation of this success.

WISDOM IS THE KEY

What exactly is wisdom? Is it a mysterious knowledge unavailable to the average person? Is it an ability to think unlocked by great amounts of higher education? Just what is wisdom and how does it work?

Not all the wisdom about life's deeper issues comes from current journals or high-tech manuals. The most important answers come from the Bible.

Although wisdom abounds in the Bible, the key book of wisdom in the Scriptures is the book of Proverbs.

Here are some exciting examples.

The Lord's wisdom founded the earth; his understanding established all the universe and space. Proverbs 3:19, TLB.

Take a lesson from the ants, you lazy fellow. Learn from their ways and be wise! For though they have no king to make them work, yet they labor hard all summer, gathering food for the winter. Proverbs 6:6-8, TLB.

If you refuse criticism you will end in poverty and disgrace; if you accept criticism you are on the road to fame. . . . Be with wise men and become wise. Be with evil men and become evil. Proverbs 13:18, 20, TLB.

Pride goes before destruction and haughtiness before a fall. . . . From a wise mind comes careful and persuasive speech. Kind words are like honey—enjoyable and healthful. Proverbs 16:18, 23-24, TLB.

If you love sleep, you will end in poverty. Stay awake, work hard, and there will be plenty to eat! Proverbs 20:13, TLB.

Steady plodding brings prosperity; hasty speculation brings poverty. Proverbs 21:5, TLB.

Do you know a hard-working man? He shall be successful and stand before kings! Proverbs 22:29, TLB.

Develop your business first before building your house. Proverbs 24:27, TLB.

A sensible man watches for problems ahead and prepares to meet them. The simpleton never looks, and suffers the consequences. The world's poorest credit risk is the man who agrees to pay a stranger's debts. Proverbs 27:12-13, TLB.

By now you get the point. This practical wisdom impacts all of life: your marriage, your children, your health, your business, your money, your relationships. This is ancient information on success you can't afford to miss.

PUTTING BIBLICAL WISOM INTO ACTION

The American economic engine of the 19th century became legend throughout the civilized world. The engine was built on solid biblical precepts such as those you have just read. And it firmly believed in the principles I've presented in this book. Dr. Richard Huber, a well-respected historian, in his landmark work, *The American Idea of Success*, states, "The best friend the idea of success ever had in the 19th century was the solid body of protestant clergymen. . . . Most Protestant clergymen poured blessings by the bucketful on the virtuous duty of accumulating wealth."

But there is so much to learn. You dread the effort. Great changes seem necessary to put biblical wisdom into action. You may not consider yourself particularly religious. Church makes you uncomfortable. Thoughts of God bring mostly nervous guilt. You want success. You want your success to be solid, based on the practical wisdom of the Bible. Yet it all seems to elude you. You just don't know how to do it.

The most important teaching of the Bible is that you have available a Friend. A cosmic ally. He is a Friend who can activate the teachings of the Bible.

He has the energy needed to make biblical success work. You probably already know his name— Jesus Christ.

The New Testament, speaking of Jesus Christ, states, "To all who received him, he gave the right to become children of God. All they needed to do was to trust him to save them" (John 1:12, TLB). It further affirms that "God loved the world so much that he gave his only Son so that anyone who believes in him shall not perish but have eternal life. God did not send his Son into the world to condemn it, but to save it." (John 3:16-17, TLB).

Wait! There's more. Jesus himself said, "Look, I have been standing at the door and I am constantly knocking. If anyone hears me calling him and opens the door, I will come in and fellowship with him and he with me" (Revelation 3:20, TLB).

This is really remarkable! If this is true, then your whole life can be wonderfully changed. You can discover who you were made to be. You can finally be on the road to genuine success. This is big stuff!

Try to forget the institutional religious baggage Jesus has been forced to carry for generations. Try hard to see who he really is.

He is God in human flesh. The Savior sent to rescue us from our own selfish, confused misery. He sacrificed himself on a cross, an instrument of execution. He gave himself in death as a substitute. A substitute for what? For you. He died to satisfy God's justice: so that you could be forgiven and brought back to your Creator, the God who intensely loves you.

The doorway to true success then is the pathway to God, and the pathway to God is a personal surrender to and relationship with God's Son, Jesus Christ.

This is simpler than you ever thought it would be. You admit your need of Jesus Christ as your Savior. You willingly turn from the self-centered control of your own life. You accept Jesus' death on the cross as a personal act for your personal benefit. You affirm your belief that Jesus Christ rose bodily from death. You finally surrender your life to the guidance and authority of God through Jesus Christ. You are now ready to learn how to intelligently study the Bible, to pray with effectiveness, and to enjoy the companionship of other men and women who share with you an amazing contact with God through a relationship with Jesus Christ.

But why bother with all the spiritual stuff? Can't you succeed without it? You can certainly make a lot of money without any thought of God. People do it every day. But, remember, we're talking about success here. Success in every part of your life. Money just isn't enough. It never is.

I believe you need a success rooted in your relationship with Jesus Christ for three reasons:

1. Success rooted in Christ will give you the opportunity to build success in all of your life—and God's Holy Spirit will help you do it!

2. Success rooted in Christ will protect your achievements from the ravages of sinful choices.

Your financial, family, and spiritual successes can increase. You are much less likely to lose because of decisions that are in violation of God's basic principles of life. You will operate with greater wisdom.

3. You're all his anyway. "The earth belongs to God! Everything in all the world is his!" (Psalm 24:1, TLB).

He is stronger than the greatest government. He has more power than all nuclear arsenals combined. He is simply Almighty God. He wrote the book on true success. He can teach you more than the most sophisticated success manuals. He is God.

You can trust him. You can love him. You can know him. He himself is the spiritual secret of true success.

OTHER BOOKS
BY
DEXTER AND BIRDIE YAGER

Don't Let Anybody Steal Your Dream
Dexter Yager with Douglas Wead

This classic in the field of motivational writing has sold more than a million copies and is selling as well today as it did in 1978 when it was first published. Dexter Yager has influenced millions with his forthright honesty, compassion and desire to see others succeed. Here is a man who has "made it" in all the right ways, and who is willing to pour out the ideas that make for successful living.

Paperback: $3.95
Hardback: $6.95

Tales of the Super Rich!
Dexter Yager and Doug Wead

This is the ultimate dream book! If you've forgotten how to dream, this will get you started on the road to rainbows.

To conduct Beethoven after supper with an ivory-and-diamond baton, Baron Alfred Rothschild kept an entire symphony orchestra on call.

The granddaughter of old Commodore Cornelius Vanderbilt loved purple. She invariable dressed in a lavender dress, carried a bunch of hothouse violets, and motored about in a silver-and-violet Rolls Royce.

During the Spanish-American War, Mrs. Jay Gould sent the United States a $100,000 bank draft to use "any way you can to get this war over and our boys home!" Not content with merely influencing politics, Mrs. Gould single-handedly turned one of her elegant homes into a hospital for returning injured soldiers.

To celebrate the storybook wedding of Prince Ranier, Aristotle Onassis showered Monaco with thousands of red carnations, gave Princess Grace an exquisite diamond necklace, and donated one million francs to one of the Prince's favorite charities. It was said to have been a most satisfactory wedding gift.

Paperback: $4.95

Becoming Rich
Dexter Yager and Doug Wead

Inspirational and moving stories of some of the world's greatest people and the eleven principles behind their success. Includes Walt Disney, Albert Einstein, Martin Luther King, Andrew Carnegie, Adoph Ochs, Jackie Robinson, Thomas Edison, Helen Keller, Harry Truman, Coco Chanel, Winston Churchill, Arturo Toscanini, and Douglas MacArthur.

Paperback: $4.95

The Secret of Living Is Giving
Birdie Yager with Gloria Wead

Birdie Yager, wife of one of America's most famous and powerful businessmen, talks about:
- Marriage: How to make it work.
- Attitude: The way to popularity and self-esteem.
- Your Husband: How to make him rich!
- Children: When to say no, and when to say yes.
- Health and Beauty: They are result of our decisions, and are not automatic.
- Money: When it is bad; when it can be wonderful.
- Faith in God: Why you must deal with your guilt and inferiority, or self-destruct.

Paperback: $3.95

The Magic Makers:
How to be Successful with People and Money
Compiled by Dexter Yager and Doug Wead

Seventeen of America's leading businessmen and women share their secrets for success. Learn how to: turn your dreams into profit; save money and invest it wisely; improve your marriage; gain the respect of your children; develop quality friendships; find faith and allow it to bring you happiness.

Included are: Fred and Linda Harteis, Jerry and Cherry Meadows, Theron and Darlene Nelson, Jim and Bev Kinsler, Jack and Debbie Kronz, Jim and Connie Agard, Bill and Hona Childers, Tony and Sue Renard, Ron and Toby Hale, Hal and Susan Gooch, Gary and Diane Reasons, Bob and Kay Goshen, Jack and Effie Reid, Bob and Irene Bolin, Hank and Alicia Gilewicz, Jerry and Barb Nelson, Fred and Pat Setzer.

Paperback: $4.95

Millionaire Mentality
Dexter Yager with Doug Wead

At last! A book on financial responsibility by one of America's financial wizards, Dexter Yager! Dexter gives freely of his remarkable business acumen, teaching you how to take inventory and plan for financial independence.

Here is a common sense, down-to-earth book about investments, shopping, credit and car buying, and budgeting time and money.

Included are anecdotes about other successful American business people—to give you ideas about where to go from here!

If you are serious about financial planning, this is the book for you!

Paperback: $4.95

The Business Handbook
Dexter Yager

The most comprehensive how-to-do-it manual ever offered!

A simple yet detailed guide that lets you chart your own path to success in Amway.

The Business Handbook brings you the best in proven techniques regardless of whether you want to earn just a little extra income or if you are interested in building a large successful organization.

Discover what MLM or Network Marketing (as revealed in Megatrends) really is and how it differs from Direct Marketing and Pyramiding.

Awaken yourself to the proven advantages offered through the Amway phenomenon.

Learn the importance of:
• Winning
• Leadership
• Goalsetting
• Loyalty
• Dreambuilding

Discover the secret techniques used by many successful distributors who have become millionaires and are fulfilling their greatest dreams.

Paperback: $6.95

Successful Family Ties: Developing Right Relationships for Lasting Success
Ron Ball with Dexter Yager

Right relationships with the people around you are fundamental to your success in life—emotionally, spiritually, and even in your work. This book will give you high-performance, practical guidelines for dealing with the many important issues that may be holding you back from experiencing success in your family relationships. You'll learn to recognize the signs of trouble and to take steps toward overcoming:

- ruptured relationships
- busy signals in communication
- sexual temptation
- stress
- selfishness
- negative people

And with principles founded on God-given, timeless truths you'll discover lasting success in all your challenges and be sure to have successful family ties.

Hardback: $10.95

Available from your distributor, local bookstore, or write to:

Freedom Distributing Company
P.O. Box 1110
Pineville, NC 28134